Three Men on Motorcycles

The Amigos ride to Ladakh

Ketan Joshi

Cover art and design by Aditya Dhurandhar

The Great Idea

'LET'S GO FOR A RIDE!' Adi said, as he always does.

If you wake up a guy in the middle of the night with a swift kick on his backside, most people would say 'WTF!!' or 'OY' or possibly something unprintable and full of cuss words - but Adi would say 'Let's go for a ride!'. I could just imagine him waking up from a coma after 10 years, and instead of asking 'What year is it?' or 'Where am I?' he would shock the doctor by saying 'Put down that stethoscope man, let's go for a ride.'

I squinted at him through the bottom of my glass. There was something wrong with my glass.

Then I realised the problem. The glass was empty.

Managerial action was required to solve the problem, and I provided the breakthrough leadership required to solve the problem by lifting the Old monk and refilling my glass.

I looked at Adi again - I didn't have much of a choice – he filled the view, as he was a giant 100 kilo monster, covered with hair. Long hair, long beard, long moustache… only his nose protruded through his moustache and beard, like a bare mountain top rising above a dense jungle. He looked like a cross between a Yeti and a shaggy sheepdog.

'AHEM HRM HRRRM' a stern sound came from the other side of the room – a reminder to pass the bottle and not keep it stuck to my greedy mitts. It came from another 100 kg monster in the room – Delzad, the mad bawa. What little space there was in the room not filled by Adi was filled by Delzad. He competed with Adi in the hair department. Though not as long as Adi's, his hair was curly and nylon-hard and was of an unusual quality - a mix of Scrubbing brushes, Desert cacti, Afro rockers and Medusa.

I was the third 100 kilo member of this weighty triumvirate, and though I did not share their impressive height, I had them beat with my waistline. The floor creaked and groaned when we three were together.

'Guys, come on – Let's go for a ride' said Adi again. He was like a broken record, but now that both our glasses were full, I and Del looked at him indulgently.

'Where should we go?' I asked.

'We can go to Konkan, or Lonar, or Nasik...' Adi started babbling

'Let's go off-roading' Delzad suddenly shouted, splashing his drink in excitement. I and Adi groaned – bawa was off on his favourite topic again. He believes that the only real riding is on stones and rocks and mud, and nice black top roads are only for wimps. Wherever he goes, he looks for a patch of bad road to ride on. Where normal people groan and slow down, bawa screams in delight and speeds up. We would be riding peacefully on a nice road and look in the mirror and see that bawa had vanished! We would stop the bike in panic and look around, and see bawa riding in the gutter by the side of the road.

'Let's leave in the middle of the night ' screamed bawa as his excitement mounted with each word he spoke 'Let's disconnect our headlights and ride in complete darkness! Let's ride into the mountains in the night! Let's jump from crag to crag like mountain goats on steroids! Let's do a wheelie right up to the top of the mountain and then do a stoppee right on the peak! Let's jump right off the peak...OW!' he stopped as I whacked him on the side of the head. 'What was that for...OW!' he stopped again as Adi whacked him on the other side of the head, and he sulked and shut up as we both glared at him

'As I was saying' Adi continued, still glaring at Bawa 'Let's go for a ride...'

'We get that bro...' I said 'But you are generally spouting names of all kinds of destinations – beaches, mountains, plains... Where do you want to go?'

'Anywhere is fine...I just want to ride.' Adi is Mr Perpetual Motion. I think he imagines that the bike is a gigantic dildo vibrator, and he gets a sexual high as his ass gets vibrated on the 500cc engine. He upgraded from some shitty plastic bike to the 500cc metal monster of a Bullet. He claims that it was for the power, but we strongly suspect that it was because of the vibration. On a long ride, he suddenly shivers, closes his eyes and moans for some reason; and then he cries 'YAHOO' and zooms off.

'Bah! All of you are wimps!' suddenly a voice sounded, and three heads swivelled in that direction.

It was Bharathi – She Who Must Be Obeyed! Though only hobbit-sized herself, she roars and emits flames like a Dragon. The whole world quails in front of her and rolls up into a ball and shivers when she unveils her glittering eye. She rules over the home with an iron fist.

She is a great adventurer and traveller, master of the four directions and the seven seas and the misty mountains! Her passion is travel and she has been everywhere and done everything! She can reel off all stations of Indian Railways, all major airports of the world, all peaks of the Himalayas, all airline codes of every plane that ever flew. Wake her up in the middle of the night and ask her about a flight from Helsinki to Honolulu and she will reel off all airlines, all fares, all visa rules and then tell you that there are many better options if you route through Hamburg rather than Heathrow.

Apart from booking tickets, her main hobby is to mock other people's travel plans. Anybody who even mentions anything about a travel plan cannot escape her. She will promptly catch them, fix them with a glittering eye, scoff at their feeble travel ambitions, lecture them about the myriad destinations and options and book their tickets for them, even as they shout and scream that they had merely asked and had no intention of going anywhere and had no leaves and no money and no passport and no visa. I am sure that in every country of the world you will find some glum Indians who had just had a casual conversation with Bharathi the day before and had just woken up dazedly and were wondering how on earth they got here.

'Why do you say 'wimps'?' I asked with dignity. 'We are talking about a manly and adventurous activity – long distance biking!'

She just made an insulting noise - like a cork coming out of a bottle.

'Manly! Ha! The manly thing to do is to ride a bicycle, not a motorcycle. And long distance? Phurrrrrr! 300 – 400 km is not long distance. You should do at least 2000 KM to call it long distance.'

'In the first place – cycling is not manly, it is merely archaic.' I replied. 'Why do think they invented the motor in the motorcycle in the first place? And where do YOU suggest we should go?' I asked.

I knew I shouldn't have needled her. She has a habit of shaking people up, and making them question the way they are living their lives. My life is pretty well shaken up by now, so I am used to it – but now Bawa and Adi's lives were about to be stirred up.

'Ladakh, of course!' she said. 'Call yourselves bikers? Then go to Ladakh!'

Ladakh, as you might know, is the high mountainous region at the extreme North of India, and is part of the Great Tibetan plateau - the roof the world! It is a wild and untamed land, a high altitude Himalayan desert with lots of high passes which are snow covered for 9 months of the year. It is the iconic ride of India, and we would have always wanted to go there and never have had the guts to actually go.

When people do go, they generally travel in a big group and have a backup vehicle and a mechanic and sometimes even a doctor with them. The roads can be in pretty bad condition, and if you have an accident or a bike breakdown you would be in deep shit. Not to mention avalanches, snowdrifts, Pakistani attacks, abominable snowmen, having to eat Maggi all the time…the dangers are many.

So for just the three of us to go was a bit of a challenge.

Another challenge which all men face is to get leave. It is when you apply for leave from work, that you learn how important you are to the running of the company. Why - the place would break down and burn to the ground if you are not around! Indian corporates will give you leave to get married, and perhaps if some family member dies - both of which can happen only a limited amount of times. To get leave for something as frivolous as a motorbiking trip - that would be a long shot indeed.

But Bharathi being involved caused magic to happen.

'You can do anything if you want it bad enough.' Is her motto.

And sure enough, everything worked out.

Adi works as a wage slave in some software company - a code factory which employs millions and doesn't believe in giving any of them any leave. The boss would explode with a loud bang when people asked for leave, and strong men would shiver like leaves in the wind when asking for holidays. Adi didn't know whom to be more afraid of - Bharathi or his boss! But one look at Bharathi convinced him that she was more fearsome and so he squared his shoulders and combed his beard and tremblingly put in a leave request.

But it was a miracle! The boss frowned terribly when he saw the leave request and Adi almost shat his pants; but when his boss found out that he wanted leave to go for a motorcycle trip to Ladakh, he became so happy that he granted it immediately. 'I always wanted to ride to Ladakh' he said tearfully 'but I could never manage it. Go for it, my boy – do it for me as well..boohoohoohoo...do it for all of those who are trapped in the cage of routine existence - we cubicle dwellers, we wife-oppressed people....booohooohoo.' he sobbed into his hanky as he signed the leave application and a bewildered but happy Adi reported the news to a smug Bharathi.

Bawa had a much tougher boss to convince – his dad! He worked in his own business with his dad, and pretty much lived with his nose to his grindstone. He lived in the same house as his boss after all! So when he applied for leave, his dad fixed him with a sardonic eye and muttered parsi comments about wastrels and layabouts and people who went traipsing about and saddled their poor old dads with double the work.

But essentially the same process applied – 'I could not do it when I was young, so I will let my son do what I could not do myself' the senior bawaji must have thought 'and though he is a lazy layabout with a thoroughly disreputable bunch of friends – especially that fat old bugger with the crazy wife – I will let him do this'

I did a much simpler thing – I just didn't tell my boss that I was going. Why trouble the poor fellow unnecessarily? What the eye don't see, the heart don't fret over. I would remotely manage the work and manage the team through phone calls and emails. It would be same thing as 'work from home' - except that I would not be home.

Preparation time!

'Let's plan the spares and repair equipment!' sang out Adi, with all the enthu of a teenage girl going shopping.

'Yes, let's!' agreed Delzad, rubbing his palms together and licking his lips.

Both of them started jumping up and down and shrieking with excitement! 'EEEEE...we will buy tyre tubes...and ball bearings....and clutch cables....and accelerator cables....and tube puncture patches....and puncture kits....and air pumps....and WD40.....and big screwdrivers and small screwdrivers ....and spark plugs....and cable ties....'

Both linked elbows and started circling around, hyperventilating with pleasure.

'...And air filters....and engine oil....and brake oil....and pliers....and fuses...'

'I will install Ladakh carrier on my bike!'

'EEEEEEEEE....WHAT FUN.....I will install a USB charging port on my bike!'

'OOOOO....THAT'S GREAT.....I will get my ass greased so that you can slide right in!!'

Ok – Adi didn't say that, but he might well have. They were so excited that they would have done anything.

They saw me looking at them with a cynical smirk, and they smirked right back.

'This fatso doesn't know what we are talking about.'

'Yeah, but when he has a breakdown he will smile the other side of his face!' Adi said

'Eh?' Bawa was confused. 'What?'

'Smile the other side of his face....means an upside down smile...' Adi explained to him.

'Upside down? He will be upside down? You mean he will have an accident and fall over? Or will he be doing yoga and standing on his head?'

Adi slapped his forehead. 'No baba....its a simile...smile upside down means that he will frown....'

'How can a smile upside down be a frown?'

'I mean – it will be a sad face....oh never mind! I mean that if he has a breakdown then he will realise the importance of what we are going to carry.'

'OOOH OOOOH OOOH.... I just remembered....we will get a tyre pressure gauge!'

'YES YES YES…..and a multimeter and ammeter and battery charger!'

'AND SOME WAX POLISH TO KEEP THE BIKES SHINY!'

'EEEEEEEEEEEEEEEE' both of them started jumping up and down in excitement again.

I shook my head and left the room.

My entire cold weather wardrobe consisted of a single sweater and a fleece jacket. I was looking at it doubtfully when Bharathi came into the room.

'That's all you need!' Bharathi announced grandly. 'When I climbed Mount Chibaba, the only thing I had was a small hankerchief. Only real losers need sweaters and warm clothes and all that crap. Look at the great rishis – they walk around dressed only a loincloth in the icy Himalayas! All it needs is breath control...'

The simple way to make her change her position is to make a statement in the opposite direction to what you want. Automatically she will change her position so that it will be of opposite to your last statement. It is instinctive - as far as she is concerned, whatever you say is wrong.

So I said 'I don't think that Ladakh will be cold. I will just carry a couple of T-shirts.'

Immediately and without any visible effort, she changed her position by 180 degrees. 'ARE YOU CRAZY? You will be crossing so many high Himalayan passes – and it might snow...it might hail...there might be glaciers and freezing winds and icebergs and snowdrifts and rain and slush and yetis and abominable snowmen....you will freeze into a solid block of ice and fall off the bike and shatter into fragments like the Terminator...what will you do without me to give you advice re.....ooh, these males I tell you...GO AND BUY SOME WARM CLOTHES AT ONCE!'

Mission accomplished.

The same stratagem worked for the packing too. 'Please don't touch my bag!' I told Bharathi 'Don't you dare to touch my bag. I will pack my bag myself!' and obviously she threw me out of the room and packed my bag nicely as I was enjoying a beer with the 2 guys.

'How did you get her to pack your bags?' Adi asked me enviously.

'Oh simple!' I said, glancing behind to see that she was out of earshot. 'I am the head of the household after all. My word is law.'

I really enjoyed the admiring looks they gave me.

The only thing left now was to choose a cool name for ourselves.

Mostly Royal Enfield riders like to travel in huge packs - from 20 to 50 bikers at a time, and though they are mostly composed of inoffensive city folk - software engineers and suchlike - they like to think of themselves as tough motorcycle gangs and wear bandannas and T shirts with pictures of skulls and crossbones on them, and give themselves aggressive names like Bandits, Pirates, Bisons, Bulls etc.

We were just three people, but we also wanted a cool name for ourselves.

Since there were only three of us, I thought of calling ourselves the 'Trinity' – but we couldn't decide who should be the father, the son and the holy ghost. Then we thought of Trimurti – but nobody wanted to be Brahma. 'What about 'Tridev'?' I asked, and all of us chanted in unison –'PAAP SE DHARTI FATEEE....FATEEE...FATEEE' but Bharathi recoiled at this.

Finally we decided on the 3 AMIGOS. Adi and Del agreed because it had the 'three' part; and 'Amigos' sounded vaguely firangi and classy.

Bike preparation

'Let's do the bike preparation!' Adi said

'Yes, Let's!' Delzad said, giggling with excitement.

'Let's change the tyres!'

'And the seats!'

'And the exhaust!'

'And the handlebars!'

'And the lights!'

'And the shock absorbers!'

'And the Air filter!'

'EEEEEEEE!!' Adi hugged himself with joy 'I will install rear leg guards!'

'OOOOOOO! I will install a power point from the battery!'

' OH OH OH.....' Adi had a major hard on. 'I WILL INSTALL LED LIGHTS!!! OOOOH...'

'LETS REMAP THE ECU!!' and both of them screamed in ecstasy and had a mutual orgasm there and then. Both collapsed weakly on the ground and lay there breathing heavily.

Me and Bharathi were looking at them in disbelief.

'So what are you going to do to your bike?' Adi asked, as he got up stiffly.

'Nothing.' I replied.

'NOTHING?!' Adi and Del looked at me in shock.

'I just bought the damn bike! What is there to do?'

'Change the seat at least...' Adi pleaded. 'Go to Perfect and get Irfan to put a new soft seat for your gargantuan ass.'

'Er...no thanks. I am fine with the stock seat.'

'Change the exhaust at least.' Del pleaded in his turn 'You can't be seen in public with the stock exhaust. Think of us, if not for you....our street cred will vanish if we are seen with a guy with a stock exhaust...'

'Yes...the new Enfield exhaust has no thump! You gotta have the THUMP!' Adi agreed. 'How can we be seen with a wimp with a wimpy exhaust?'

'Oh fuck off.' I brushed them aside 'It's a fucking brand new bike! Why does it need a new exhaust? Anyway, all the authorities say that you should keep the bike as stock as possible before a long ride.'

Adi and Del looked at each other and nodded at each other. Moving as quick as hairy lightning, Adi grabbed me and held me immobile in a bear hug, while Del snatched my bike key and ran off and all I heard was a soft purring as they took my bike and zoomed off in a cloud of dust.

The next time I saw the bike, it had a new short exhaust which made a loud 'BHADBHADBHADBHAD' noise which scared the birds for miles around!

'Now at least you won't embarrass us when we are seen in public together.' Said Adi smugly as I looked at my bike in disbelief. 'You are a fat embarrassment, but at least your bike has street cred.'

Finally everything was done, and we were all ready to start the ride.

We could either ride the bikes all the way from Mumbai to Leh or we could transport the bikes from Mumbai to Chandigarh and ride from there.

The hardcore rider's view was to ride all the way from Mumbai.

'The moment you load your bike onto a train, is the moment you stop being a biker.' One guy told me. 'A true biker will ride his bike all the way.'

'The moment I listen to your stupid advice is the moment I stop being sane' I told him. 'Do the world a favour and go fuck yourself. Do you think I have no better things to do in life than to ride 2000 kilometres of straight and boring highway in blazing summer? Chutiya sala.'

So we decided to transport the bikes. The easiest option would be send the bikes through a courier. The courier guy would come to your house and pick up the bike and send the bike by truck. We could pick it up at the courier office in Chandigarh. Zero pain. But Bharathi sneered at this.

'It will take at least a week for your bikes to reach by road.' She said 'and they will load all kinds of stuff on top of your bikes and screw them. And it will be expensive. It would be much better to send the bikes by train. You will get the bikes in Chandigarh the very next day.'

None of us had ever sent anything by train before, so we went to the station to figure out how it is done. It is simple enough - you come to the station with your documents - Registration, insurance and 'Pollution under control' certificates and book your bike on the train. If you are also travelling on the same train, then you can book it as your 'luggage', and if you are not, then you can book it as a 'parcel'. Luggage is more expensive than parcel, because it will definitely be loaded as your luggage, while a parcel is freight and can be offloaded if more important freight gets booked on the train. So if you want to be hundred percent sure to get your bike on time, then pay the extra money and book it as luggage. And buy a ticket on the train of course.

You need to pack your bike nicely to prevent dings and dents, and it is compulsory to empty the bike of all petrol, and then it is your responsibility to get some coolies to load the bike in the freight car. You can do it all yourself, but it is easier to leave it to a parcel agent who will do all the running around for a modest fee.

We went to the station and met the parcel agent who did the bike loading and reserved our space – the luggage space is limited on a train, and if a few other people also decided to go at the same time, then we would be left high and dry.

We booked flight tickets for ourselves, and the day before the flight we went to the station to despatch the bikes. The agent met us and collected the paperwork and removed all the petrol from the bikes. He started to pack the bikes, but bawa said No! He would pack his bike himself!

He had brought enough packaging material to pack an entire bus load of bikes and he and Adi started packing the first bike very lovingly. They did an excellent job and packed it with bubble wrap and paper and cardboard and cotton and clouds and stardust and Kevlar and reinforced concrete and took 2 hours to pack a single bike. The agent watched this with disillusionment and then observed that since the train was due in just a few hours, it would be better if they packed the bikes themselves. Del and Adi were exhausted by that time, so they agreed and watched while the agent's packing boys wrapped up the other 2 bikes in 10 minutes flat!

After making the agent swear on his mother's grave that the bikes would be properly and carefully loaded in the train the next day, we left for the night. The agent looked exhausted and must have been really happy to see us go.

So now the dice were cast! The Rubicon had been crossed! The bikes had gone!

There was no turning back now – We were definitely on our way to Ladakh!

Mumbai to Chandigarh

We met at the airport the next day, all weighed down with saddlebags and backpacks and helmets and stuff. Me and Adi came in first - we were well in time for the flight and looked happily at the short check in queue and our fairly low luggage. And then we waited and waited and waited for bawa to turn up and started chewing our fingernails, then our fingers and then our knuckles as the time to flight became shorter and shorter and the check in line grew longer and longer. Finally bawa came rushing in huffing and puffing and carrying a giant saddlebag which seemed to weigh as much he did. He was carrying all the repair equipment – tyre tubes and screw drivers and air pump and all that stuff, and we had a difficult job convincing the airline not to bill us an arm and a leg for extra baggage fees.

But the Indigo people were good people and they finally let us in without billing us extra. And the check-in girl was cute too. Go Indigo!

'It was my natural sexual magnetism that saved us.' Adi announced grandly. 'Just one friendly smile from me and she went weak at the knees.'

'Balls.' Retorted Del 'Your creepy sex-offender smile scared her so much she stamped us in as fast as she could so that you and your foul beard would leave as soon as possible.'

'Never mind re...' I consoled the offended Adi 'Either way it was your imposing personality that saved us.'

'It was my winning smile and sexual magnetism I tell you...' he was insisting as well came to the security check. I cleared it easily, but seeing the giant forms of Adi and Del looming behind me, the security guy immediately blew a fuse. They looked like an overweight death squad. Goyle and Crabbe came to mind, but then I was so embarrassed at making Harry Potter references, that I immediately put it out of my mind. They had to endure a detailed pat down before the CISF reluctantly released them. They were lucky to get off without an anal cavity search.

I grinned as Adi came up scowling. 'Looks like your natural sexual magnetism backfired big boy. What did you do? Gave him a winning smile?'

We got on the plane and had a bit of a struggle about who will take which seat, but I jockeyed my superior weight and managed to claim the window seat. Adi claimed to have a weak bladder and weak bowels and so claimed the aisle seat and bawa scowlingly sat in the middle.

'Air travel makes me queasy, I warn you' he said 'if the flight is rough, I will puke over both of you.'

'Oooh..how nice.' Adi squealed and clapped his hands 'It makes me queasy too! The slightest air pocket will have me retching! Maybe we will be sick together and puke all over this fat fuck.'

And sure enough, just the motion of the plane taxiing from the parking spot made them go a bit green and shut up. And these are the guys who revel in riding on the roughest roads they can find! Weird people.

The pre-flight rituals started - the pilot made his usual boring and pointless speech which no one is ever interested in, the air-hostess started the safety briefing which no human has ever paid any attention to; and just as the plane was about to take off - my phone started ringing! Shit, I had forgotten to put it off. The air hostess glared at me and looked so much like an angry schoolteacher, that I shrivelled and didn't dare to take the call. I just muted it and let it ring out. After the basilisk-glare aunty had gone, I surreptitiously checked my phone and saw that Truecaller had identified it.

'Hmm. That's odd.' I muttered.

'What?' Adi asked.

'Apparently I have just missed a call from Mumbai Airport security. How strange. Why should Mumbai Airport Security be calling me?'

'Oh Shit Oh Shit Oh Shit Oh Shit!' Bawa wailed, and we looked at him in surprise.

'What?'

'How will I show my face in the agiary again? What will I say to the Bawa samaj? How can I hold my shaggy head up in Parsi colony again? What will my dad say? Boohooohooohooo.'

Adi and me looked at each other questioningly but shrugged at each other.

'Kya hua be? Why are you wailing and weeping and beating your breast like that?'

'Arre...I have grass in my bag. Oh no Oh no Oh no Oh no'

Adi went pale and began to sweat, but I was unperturbed.

'So?'

'What do you mean 'so'? The dogs must have sniffed it out...the cops must be on guard....the DEA must have issued a red corner alert for us…they must have alerted Chandigarh security….3 big sardarji policemen will arrest us…they will march us to jail and beat us up….they will probably sodomise us once they are through with beating us…..BOO HOO HOO… I AM GOING TO DIE OF AIDSSSSSSS….'

'Here – relax!' I said soothingly. 'No one cares about a bit of grass. There are no dogs at the domestic airport. And even if he had found a small bag of grass, the only thing he would do is to whack it and take it home and toke up himself. Chill man.'

'Easy for you to say.' Del continued to sob. 'You don't have any stuff in your possession.'

'Of course I do' I said and took a packet out of my pocket and showed it to them 'See?'

Their eyes became four round 'o's and mouths were another two 'O's as they stared at the bag of booti.

'What shit! You are carrying that stuff around with you? In a plane?!!!'

'Yeah…that's what I am telling you…no one cares. Especially not for such tiny amounts.'

'SHIT SHIT SHIT' Adi slumped back in his seat. 'One guy has the shit in his bags – the other guy has it on his person! For no fault of mine I am going to end up in the clink'

As usual I fell asleep in the flight and was fresh and relaxed when we landed, but both of them were looking wan and tired. They both had sat bolt upright in their seats for the whole of the flight, shivering with tension and looking nervously at the flight attendants every time they came near, just in case Mumbai Airport Security had radioed the plane to arrest the miscreants and stun them and handcuff them or something.

They were as jumpy as cats in a dog show at the airport and turned pale and started farting every time a policeman even looked in their direction. When the bags finally came on the baggage carousel, bawa turned even more pale and grabbed my hand and hissed 'Look!'

His bag had an official sticker on it. 'Opened and resealed by Airport security'

'They searched my bag!' he quavered.

'Oh yeah....your bag has all kinds of lethal screw drivers and bike parts in it, so they must have checked it. That's why they called – they probably wanted to ask what was in it, and when we didn't answer, they opened the bags themselves.'

In spite of my explanation, they were still deeply nervous and didn't dare say a word until we were in a taxi and en route to the railway station.

At the railway station, luckily the process of getting the bikes was extremely straightforward. I stayed outside with the bags while Adi and Bawa went inside – showed the railway receipt and bike documents and collected the bike and wheeled them outside.

The railways and the police have two opposing rules. The railways are concerned about safety and fire hazards and are extremely strict about the bike petrol tank being completely empty – not even a drop is allowed to be there in the tank. The reason for this is simple – a bike may fall, the petrol may leak and a fire may result – and a fire in a running train is the worst thing that could happen. So there is not even a drop of petrol in the vehicle.

The police on the other hand, do not allow Petrol to be sold loose in a bottle. The reason for this is known only to themselves. Possibly they are concerned about people making petrol bombs or immolating themselves or somebody else or perhaps black-marketing petrol. All these reasons would have been valid except for one simple point – if I wanted to do any of these things, I would fill up petrol in my bike, go out of the petrol pump and promptly take the petrol out of the vehicle and do whatever illegal thing I wished to do.

But the police enforce this stupid rule very strictly all over India – no pump will sell you petrol in a bottle. Even if you have run out of petrol on the highway and just need a bottle to enable you to get your vehicle to the nearest petrol pump – they just shrug their shoulders. No way, Jose. No petrol in a bottle.

If anybody from the Police who made this damn fool rule is reading this – Here's a message from me - Go fuck yourself! You are an asshole.

I hope that your vehicle breaks down on the highway and no one gives you even a drop of fuel and you have to push your bike for miles and miles up a steep slope. Morons. Idiots. Fools.

But then, we are intelligent people. We solve problems. And we solved this problem by getting a local Chandigarh based friend to fill up his bike with petrol and meet us at the station.

That friend was the crazy laughing serd – JP Singh. JP had a touring company called Motomonks, which organises Ladakh bike tours for tourists. So for the season he was based in Chandigarh and took a bunch of riders up the mountains every now and then. He had done the Manali Leh ride so many times that he was heartily sick of motorcycling and had stopped biking altogether. Nowadays he wears shorts and chappals and sits in the support vehicles instead of biking.

He rolled up in his Bullet and we took the petrol from his tank and filled up a litre each in ours and zoomed off to the petrol pump to fill up. Easy as pie!

We didn't even pay him for the petrol! The poor fellow. His flabber was totally gasted, as we rode off happily without even thinking of putting our hands in our pockets. He must have been muttering Punjabi gaalis into his beard, but no doubt he gained good karma by helping us. Anybody planning to go on a organised tour to Leh, please do go with JP Singh and the Motomonks. He is a good fellow. I still haven't paid him for that petrol.

We demanded JP take us to a famous local dhaba and hogged like pigs out there. We tried to make him pay for lunch as well, but he showed us the finger. And after all that, it was well past noon that we finally set out on the ride.

Just as we started riding, I suddenly braked and Delzad nearly banged into me.

'What?!' He asked, looking irritated.

'Very important task. Almost forgot' I said, and went to the liquor shop and bought six halves of old Monk rum.

'Ah very good, very good.' Delzad beamed as he patted me on the back. 'NOW we are all set. The ride starts now'.

Chandigarh to Samba

Our planned route was to enter through Jammu - Srinagar and cross over to Ladakh through the Zoji La pass, explore the Ladakh region and then exit through Manali via the Leh- Manali road.

On the first day, we were planning to hit Jammu. But what with unloading and chitchat with JP and hogging on lunch, we were very late to start that day.

Chalo, never mind – we would simply stop wherever we were at night fall. I don't like night riding, and even more so in J&K – somebody might shoot you!

We started on the ride, and WOW! I was in love with the power of the huge 500cc engine! What a rush! The brand new 500 was a distinct notch above my old 350, and I was loving it. I went VROOM VROOM and went flying over the countryside.

I hadn't had a chance to really ride the new bike – The only riding I had done on it was the initial break-in, where you are not supposed to cross 40 kph for the first 100 km and not cross 60 kph till 500 km. I had done the first service and now the engine was nicely broken in and ready to ride at full power.

I was very pleasantly shocked by the power of my machine, and once I was used to it, I really twisted that accelerator and left Adi and Del in the dust. They were quite surprised by this, because generally I am the slow rider, who chugs along gawking at the scenery.

There was no scenery to appreciate here though – Punjab is pancake flat, the roads were good and the bike was powerful. We zoomed along happily on smooth roads.

Suddenly we saw a big group of people on the road, stopping vehicles and shoving things at them.

The difference in our reactions was interesting.

Adi – 'I want perpetual motion. The bike must be moving all the time. Why are people trying to stop me? Maybe they are zombies and want to drink my blood and eat my brains!!! Or maybe terrorists who want to shove a bomb up my ass!!! AAAARRRRRGHGHHHHHH......' And he took a steep turn, avoided the crowd and went away.

Delzad – 'Shit! Looks like some sort of problem… Maybe there has been an accident or something. Or perhaps a demonstration of some kind. Maybe a biker hit someone and ran away and now they want to beat up all bikers who pass by. BUT THEY CANNOT CATCH ME. I AM THE GHOST RIDER!!! AAAAAAAAAARGGHHH....' and he took a steep turn and zoomed off.

Myself – 'I wonder what's going on....what a strangely heterogenous crowd...sardarjis and non sardarji….ooh...cute chick with nice hair and a nice ass.... oh no, it's a fat bearded sardar with his hair open....what a disappointment...oh they are distributing something to eat! Fantastic, let's stop.' And I stopped and one kid came and thrust a glass into my hand. I opened my helmet visor and sniffed at it – it smelt good, so I drank it. It was a pleasant sugary drink. It was extremely refreshing, just right for that muggy hot day.

'What's going on brother?' I asked 'Is it some religious day or something? Why are you distributing water on the road?'

'No, nothing like that. Its very hot, so we are doing good deeds by giving water to passers-by....STOP THAT TRUCKWALA, HE IS GETTING AWAY!!' he suddenly screamed, startling me exceedingly. He ran after that truck and jumped up and yanked the cabin door open. The truck driver must have shat in his pants, thinking that he is going to get beaten up for sure. You could see the wonder and relief in eyes when instead of a punch in the face, he was offered a glass of sherbet.

What violent social service, I thought, and had another glass of sherbet before leaving.

Del and Adi were waiting nervously some distance ahead. They were sure that I had been captured and was being beaten within an inch of my life or something and were wondering whether they should call the police or an ambulance or ride back to rescue me.

They were arguing as to which number to call when I came up

'Call 911 I tell you!'

'Bastard, are you in US or what? Call 100'

'Bugger, that's only in Bombay. And I think that's only from land line.'

'Maybe its 104'

'That's the senior citizen helpline I think' Adi said doubtfully.

'That fat fucker is a senior citizen only....ah there he is'

They were relieved to see me safe and sound, and were a bit embarrassed that they were scared shitless by a group of social workers distributing water. They resolved to stop at all such stops in the future, as it was indeed bloody hot. While riding it was fine, but as soon as you stop, it was hot and humid.

We passed through Punjab and in the late evening entered the state of Jammu and Kashmir. There was a huge line of cars and trucks stuck at the entry point toll booth, but since we were on bikes we just breezed through. Two and three wheelers don't have to pay highway tolls in India, so we don't get stuck in traffic at toll points and just pass them by, sticking our tongues out and thumbing our noses at them.

We had planned to hit Udhampur for the night, but it was already getting late and I wasn't particularly enthusiastic about riding in the dark. We would have to find some midway place to stay in.

Adi was shitting bricks! Someone had told him that someone or the other shoots you if you ride in the dark. It might be terrorists, or BSF or Army or Home Guards, or NCC or Boy Scouts or anyone - but he was convinced that someone would shoot him.

'Come on man – no one is going to shoot you' I consoled him.

'Yeah...' Delzad agreed. 'More likely that there will be a bomb in the road.'

'A bomb!' Adi squeaked. This was even worse than bullets.

'No no...' I said 'Don't be silly. The chances are much higher that a truck will bang into you in the dark.'

'A truck!' Adi squeaked again

'Oh yes! It very possible.' Del weighed in again 'if you fall beneath the wheels of a 16 wheeler, then you will be crushed so flat that they will have to scrape you off the tarmac with a spatula.'

'!!!'

I knew that there was a big turn-off to Udhampur a little way ahead, and then the road snaked through some hilly passes and jungles before coming to Udhampur. I wanted to stop before we hit that turnoff, because doing hilly passes and jungles in the night in J&K is a damn silly idea.

We passed another small town and were almost through it when I stopped. This was ridiculous. Even the smallest of towns and villages had a hotel or a lodge or a guest house or a circuit house to stay in. There had to be one here – we were just not seeing it. What one horse town was this anyway? I checked the sign – and lo and behold – the town was called 'Samba'. (Samba was the name of the sidekick of the main villain Gabbar Singh in the iconic hindi film 'Sholay'. And If you didn't know that your life sucks. Go see the film. Now. Right now.)

On cue, all of us shouted 'KITANE AADMI THE?'

'No no..' Del corrected himself 'That's the wrong dialogue for Samba'

He was right of course, so all of us again shouted 'KITNA INAAM RAKHE HAIN SARKAR HAM PAR?'

We took another breath and shouted even louder 'POORE PACHAAS HAZAAR!!'

Much refreshed by this, we went hunting for hotels. You can't go wrong by staying in a town called Samba.

We found a seedy looking hotel and knocked on the door. The hotel owner came to us looking like a minor villain - chewing on a toothpick and mentally counting notes in his head. 3 guys on big bikes in the dark meant people without much options and much money.

I asked him for a room, and he did have one. How much? I asked, and he smiled and said 2500 rupees. I was dumbfounded. '2500 bucks for this sack of shit hotel?' I told disbelievingly 'Are you crazy or what?'

He was deeply insulted. 'This is the best hotel in the district. I am talking about our crème de la crème room – AC room with attached bath. And it's a large room – it has four beds. And it has a 2 TON AC! I am the only hotel in the whole Samba district with a two ton AC!! Just come and take a look sir, and then tell me if I am right or wrong.'

Right or wrong, he was in a strong position and the room was OK. I bargained the rent down to 2k and unpacked the bikes and took the luggage up two flights to the room. We put on that 2 ton AC, ordered some grub, and opened the first bottle of Old Monk and toasted the first successful day of the ride.

We didn't hit Udhampur as planned, but all things considered, we had done very well indeed.

'YE GAAV WAALE KAUN CHAKKI KE AATE SE ROTI BANAATE HAIN RE?' I roared, biting into a leathery roti, but the two had had enough of Sholay.

'Oh fuck off.' They said and went to sleep, clutching each other.

Samba to Pahalgam

TRRRRRINNNGGGGGG – my phone went off like a bomb in my ear, shocking me awake.

'What what...who....' I frantically picked up the phone. Why was Bharathi calling at 5 in the morning? I took the call with thoughts of fire, accident, murder, earthquakes and other disasters in my head.

'H – H – Hello?'

'UTHO REY! WAKE UP! UTHO REY! WAKE UP! UTHO REY! UTHO REY! GET UP YOU LAZYBONES!'

'WTF?' she had screamed so loudly that Adi and Delzad also heard it and sat upright with a jerk. Del's hair seemed to have grown overnight and Adi's beard and head hair had got all mixed up in the night and now you couldn't make out any facial features at all – he looked like an animated fur ball.

'GET UP YOU LAZY BUGGERS, YOU SLEEPY SWINE!' she continued hollering and I just sighed and put the phone on the window. Even the MacMohan clone below must have woken up with a fright.

I had been afraid of this. As she was not here with me to nag me in person, she would be doing cyber-nagging. She would be using all the technology she knew to nag us into being the kind of traveller she wanted us to be. Phone calls, SMSs, Emails would flow with regularity. At least the advances in technology ensured that she was doing it over the airwaves, else we would be getting a pigeon every morning with a note tied to his leg, coming and crapping on my shoulder every morning and going GUTAR GOO in my ear.

'So did you reach Udhampur?'

'Er...no...we stopped at Samba'

'Lazy disgusting wretches! Why do I bother making plans for you? You must have stopped to have a huge disgusting lunch at Chandigarh, didn't you?'

'Er...yes.'

'I knew it! Get up! GET up! Get UP! GET UP AT ONCE! YOU HAVE TO REACH PEHELGAM TODAY WITHOUT ANY EXCUSES! UNDERSTOOD?' she screamed with so much authority, that all of us jumped to our feet, snapped to attention and saluted. Even the hotel owner two floors below jumped to attention and saluted.

'YES MA'M!' We shouted together and rushed to clean up and get on the bikes.

When we came down, we saw that the hotel owner was still standing rigidly at attention, saluting and trembling.

We hit the road again, and took the bypass to Udhampur, so that we could avoid Jammu town. The scenery was becoming more and more mountainous and beautiful, as we were well and truly in the Himalayan foothills. Beautiful green mountains, deep gorges with rivers, blue skies...and also a lot of traffic – so you couldn't lose yourself in the scenery, but had to keep eyes on road a lot of the time.

The railways were hard at work, building the rail line to Jammu, and it was quite startling to see a whole train coach on a truck on the road. It was a bloody humongous train on top of a humongous truck, and it had screwed the traffic for miles around. But being on two wheelers we were able to go through gaps and bypass the traffic jam.

We saw a lot of Bullets coming the opposite way – these were the guys who had started from Manali and were exiting from Jammu. They all had a set of prayer flags tied to their handlebars, and this was almost like a degree certificate of completing the Ladakh ride. The etiquette was to buy the flags only in Leh, so that you could display it proudly as a mark of your achievement - it would be a no-no to buy the flags anywhere else. We greeted each bike with a thumbs up or wave, and were cheerfully greeted in return – a mark of respect in the Bullet brotherhood.

We crossed Udhampur and stopped for lunch near the tourist spot of Patnitop, near the Chenab river. It was a beautiful spot, on a plateau in the Shivalik range.

Apparently the actual name of the place was 'Patan da talab' – meaning 'pond of the princess' The Brits couldn't pronounce it, so they garbled the name to Patni-top. We didn't see a pond or a princess, because Mr Perpetual Motion, the Yeti bulleteer, wouldn't hear of stopping anywhere or exploring anything.

'Let's move man!' was his motto. 'Let's reach that place we were supposed to reach before it gets dark'

He was still convinced that he would be shot if he rode in the dark, and wanted only to complete his journey. He wasn't intending to be a traveller, but only a biker.

And the second part was that he just couldn't remember the route – where we had been and where we were going. He just knew what we were going to Leh, and that we had come from Chandigarh and everything else was a bit of a fog. We used to quiz him every night about where he had been today and where he was supposed to be tomorrow and throw stones at him when he got it wrong. Sometimes we threw stones even when he was right, because he had no idea whether he was right or wrong. To this day, if you ask him the route, he ducks and covers his head out of sheer habit.

He carried the day, and we just breezed through Patnitop and carried on to Banihal where we encountered the famous Jawahar tunnel.

This is a very cool underground road below the Pir Panjal range, and connects the villages of Banihal and Qazigund. This is part of the road from Srinagar to Jammu, and in olden days was a high mountain pass which used to get blocked by snow and ice in the winter and be a pain to traverse. To solve this problem, they constructed an almost 3 km tunnel below the mountain, so that you can basically say 'Fuck you' to the god of the high mountain pass and pass happily below ground all year round. The first tunnel was dug in the 50's, and has since been upgraded to be a fancy four-lane tunnel with ventilation, pollution and temperature sensors and whatnot. It's an amazing thing to see and experience.

But it is also very heavily policed, as it is the most obvious terrorist target in the region. The cops promptly stopped us all and perused our papers and looked suspiciously at Adi before letting us through.

It was great fun going through the tunnel, and as soon as you come out, you saw the beautiful Kashmir valley open out in front of you. It was such a beautiful spot that everyone one stopped out there to admire the view, and the BRO had built a small parking and viewing area there so that scenery gawkers did not obstruct traffic. There were a bunch of hawkers there selling cherries in boxes and some general tourist shit. Adi promptly bought a box of cherries as a memento of our stop.

We were all enthused at entering the valley and hit the road again. A lot of people stay in Srinagar for the night, but I always thought that it was a bad idea. Srinagar is crowded, polluted, expensive, unsafe at times, full of suspicious security forces and obnoxious Indian tourists. The last time I had been in Srinagar, the place had been packed so full of Gujju tourists that the whole area around Dal lake had become strictly vegetarian.

Not that it mattered what I thought, of course. Bharathi had given us strict instructions to spend the night in Pahalgam and that's where we were going. So instead of carrying on to Srinagar, we turned at Anantnag and carried on to Pahalgam.

The first sight of Pahalgam is enchanting – you enter the Lidder valley and its like being in paradise – it is so beautiful. The Lidder is the name of the river, and it's amazingly beautiful. You see the place and you understand why Kashmir is Kashmir. Beautiful singing river, green fields, snow capped mountains – the works. But since it is such an important tourist spot, terrorists are always trying to liven up the place by chucking grenades about, so there is a pretty heavy security cover all the time.

Pahalgam was pretty much chock full of tourists and looked foul and overcrowded. But as we got away from the bus stand and main market, the crowd thinned out and we got a very nice room in a small hotel on the river side. I much prefer these small hotels to the large ones - they have more charm and personality, and are much cheaper as well.

I was quite satisfied as we stripped the luggage off the bike. We had covered almost 300 km, and were on schedule for the trip. After changing out of the biking gear we relaxed by the river side, eating the cherries that Adi had bought at the tunnel mouth.

'Look Adi' I said 'I am taking your cherry!'

'Bah.' Delzad said, spitting out a cherry pit. 'I was the first to take his cherry. You are getting sloppy seconds.'

'Fuck you, bastards' Adi responded, trying to one-up us 'I was the first one to take my own cherry – I took it before either of you.'

And then he realised what he had said, and sat there looking grumpy as we rolled on the ground, laughing our guts out.

We finished off the cherries, and then bawa grandly announced that he was going to roll a joint.

'Good.' I said 'But do you know how to do it?'

'Of course I do!' he declared confidently. 'In theory anyway. I have seen other people do it, and it looked quite easy.'

'Go for it dude' we settled down to watch the master at work.

First, he took out his stash. The whole stash consisted of one tiny little plastic pouch filled with the worst quality grass in creation. It looked more like Oregano than Marijuana.

'This?' I squinted at it in disgust 'You made such a fuss in the plane about this packet of shit? You would be a bloody disgrace as a drug dealer man.'

Bawa was outraged. He had gone to great lengths to get this packet of weed, and was feeling like some big law-breaking stud. The only law-breaking that had happened was the swindling that was done by the seller to him.

'Bugger, if you don't want it, don't take it.' He growled, and I held up my hands for peace.

'No no....go right ahead.'

'I will now clean this.' Bawa announced and tipped out a bit on a piece of paper. I peered at it. This would take some cleaning – it seemed to have more husk than weed. I went up to get the rum and offered it to Adi, but he refused. 'Don't want to mix weed with rum man.' I laughed HAHAHA. That would be an issue if bawa actually managed to put up some weed to smoke. I will stick with the rum for now.

For almost an hour Bawa sat there, picking at the weed like an old woman cleaning stones out of rice, and Adi sat there, looking like a large shaggy sheepdog dog waiting at the dinner table for scraps. The same air of expectancy, the same erect attentive posture, the same air of confusion as to what exactly was going on.

Finally, I cleared my throat and said that we better go and hunt out some place to eat, as J&K might shut early for the night. Bawa was looking wild-eyed with concentration and effort, and he had a very very small pile of finished stuff as result of his labour.

By the time we came back, Pahalgam had fallen asleep and we sat for something at the river side enjoying the night and the song of the river before we also crashed for the night.

Pahalgam to Sonamarg

TRINGGGGG. TRRRRRRRRRRINGGGGGGGGG

'What ...wha....' Adi opened one eye, and bawa just rolled over and groaned.

'UTHO RE....UTHO RE....UTHO RE....UTHO RE...GET UP YOU LAZY SWINE...RISE AND SHINE' Bharathi was in good voice this morning. I could just imagine her in her village shouting at the buffalos to come out of the water.

One shot of hearing her stentorian voice was enough to get both of them up and going as well as if I had shoved a needle up their ass.

We were supposed to ride straight to Sonamarg, but as we got on to the road, the mountains looked very inviting, so I turned to the opposite direction.

'Hey, what are you doing?' Del asked. 'Aren't we supposed to go back the way we came?' Adi didn't say anything. All roads were the same to him.

'Yeah...but just look at this' I said, gesturing around 'It's so beautiful! Let's check it out!'

'Sure. Go for it. Lead the way.' Bawa is always ready for adventure.

We went riding steadily up the mountain – it was so beautiful! The massive peaks in the distance, the cool green mountains around us, the azure blue sky, the puffy white clouds, the cool breeze while riding, the amazingly fresh air, the feel of the wind as the bikes picked up speed...

For people who keep wondering why we ride bikes, when we can travel in a car – this the reason. At times, you feel so at one with the world when you are riding, you can't get that feeling in a car. The changes in temperature as the sun plays hide and seek with clouds, the feeling of the damp as you cross a stream, the smell of vegetation as you cross a meadow or a farm, that thump of the powerful motorcycle beneath you, that feel of G force as you bend the bike as you take a steep turn...I could go on and on.

As people keep saying 'Four wheels move the body, two wheels move the soul'

Obviously there are issues as well – you might not want to be quite so close to the elements when it's cold and wet, and you might not appreciate the road when you slip and fall on it – but every rose has its thorn.

I would say to everyone – get on a bike – a powerful bike if possible, but any bike in a pinch – and go for a ride on a beautiful mountain road at least once in your life.

(Bharathi would say – do this on a bicycle instead of a motorcycle)

'So where are we and where are we going?' Del asked when we stopped to enjoy the scenery. Adi had refused to get off his bike – he was sulking about stopping.

'I don't know, but seeing the quality of the road, it definitely goes somewhere important. You wouldn't build a road like this for some tiny village.'

We kept going and I was a bit taken aback when it abruptly terminated in a crowded tented camp, surrounded by hordes of security personnel. After we dismounted and went for a cup of tea, we discovered the reason. This was one of the routes to the famous Amarnath yatra.

Amarnath is one of the major pilgrimage points in J&K, as devotees trek from Pahalgam or Sonmarg to a cave in the mountains, where there is a hunk of ice which looks like a Shiva Lingam. All ice stalagmites look similar in my opinion, but it is this cave where a big stalagmite is revered as a natural and magical Shiva lingam and hordes and hordes of gullible pilgrims risk life and limb to climb up perilous mountain paths to take a look at it. More than 7 lakh people come in a 45 day period in July – August, and this camp was there to take care of them, and the security guys were there to ensure that nobody shot them.

'SEVEN LAKH PEOPLE!' I paled. 'When are they coming?'

'Tomorrow the yatra will start' the hotel guy grinned, rubbing his hands together. 'We are expecting a bumper crop this year – I am hoping to do good business.'

'Let's get out of here fast' I said to the two Amigos. 'If the yatra is starting tomorrow then people will start coming in here today and the roads will get blocked.'

'Check out Betaab valley as you go down' the hotel guy told us as we paid our bill. 'It's a very beautiful spot where the film 'Betaab' was filmed'

Betaab valley was indeed very beautiful, and we got out of Pahalgam just in the nick of time, as I could see clouds of dust thrown up by a line of Sumos which were coming to ferry the faithful from Jammu to Pahalgam.

We backtracked back to the city of Anantnag to catch the Srinagar road, and passed the Anantnag Sun temple.

Anantnag is a very ancient city dating back to more than 7000 years ago, and this was a very ancient temple complex dedicated to Martanda, the Sun god - built about 1500 years ago. It is supposed to have had some excellent carvings and was a very major temple until it was destroyed by muslim rulers as a show of force in the 15th century. In ancient times the Indian kingdoms ruled as far away as Afghanistan and central Asia. The Mauryan empire of King Ashoka stretched from Afghanistan to Bengal. Ashokan era Hindu temples are found in the far reaches of Afghanistan and Ashokan edicts can be seen in the Kabul museum.

But over the centuries many other peoples defeated them and poured over the Khyber pass for loot and conquest- the Greeks, the Huns, the Shakas, the Mongols, the Turks, the Persians, the Afghans, the Mughals etc. Some did the loot and run thing, while others decided to stay and take over the whole place. They defeated the local kings and obviously they wanted to cow down the populace and show the locals who was boss - and what better way to do it than by screwing with their temples to show that even their gods can't save them.

But now it has now been somewhat restored and is a big tourist draw. I wanted to go in and check out the temple, but Mr Perpetual motion vroomed vroomed his disapproval and so we left it behind and continued on our way. That was a real pity - should have stopped to check it out.

The road to Srinagar turned out to be unexpectedly pleasant. At one point, the scene was so remarkable that we stopped to admire it. The trees on both sides of the road formed a perfect arch over the road, and it was known as the 'Green tunnel'. The quality of the light itself looked green and very different. We stopped there at a dhaba for a cup of tea, and Adi and Del decided to use the time for some photos.

We tried to take a photo of them lying down in the middle of the road, and they were nearly run over by an indignant truck, who screamed at them as they ran for cover.

From there it was a long run into Srinagar. As we entered Srinagar, the traffic was quite awful, with multiple security checks, speed breakers, hordes and hordes of grim faced army guys on full alert. Since we were on two wheelers, we managed to bypass the traffic and rode into town, over lots and lots of giant speed breakers and past huge traffic jams caused by said security checks.

Srinagar is like a city under siege, and I wanted to eat and get out of there. I was looking for 'Ahdoo's hotel' – I had eaten there the last time I was in Srinagar and had been totally bowled over by the taste. That food was SO GOOD! It was like your tongue is having an orgasm with every bite you take! The meat is so succulent and delicious, the spices are so different and tasty, the style of cooking is something else altogether! As a dedicated foodie and cuisine explorer, I can put hand on heart and tell you sincerely that Kashmiri food is one the finest food that I have ever eaten.

As I was standing in the chowk, trying to connect to Google maps to find the way to the hotel, I was seen by a local Kashmiri Bulleteer. His face lit up when he saw me in full riding gear and saddlebags and he immediately came across to share pleasantries and ask about my trip. I was also very happy to meet a Bullet brother in a strange city and chatted with him and he actually went out of his way and guided me to Ahdoo's.

If you are on a Bullet, you will find friends everywhere.

The hotel seemed to be much busier than what it was the last time I visited, and the food was still excellent. I told the waiter that we had had some Kashmiri food the night before. Really, where? He asked and smirked indulgently when I admitted that it was in some no-name roadside stall in Pahalgam.

'Just wait until you taste OUR food sir' he replied. 'You will that it is very different from roadside food.'

We ordered Roganjosh and Yakhni and Aab Gosht and Goshtaba and whatever else there was on the menu. That cook must have started sweating looking at the order, and must have promptly screamed at the butcher to kill the rest of his flock pronto. The waiters strained and sweated under the load and the table groaned under the weight of the food.

And what food!

It was delicious. Food depends on three things - quality of the ingredients, quality of the recipe and quality of the chef - and when all three are winners, the only thing left is to get a good quality of eaters. And boy, did we qualify in that regard. We ate and ate and ate until even the big eating kashmiri locals were impressed.

I dream of attending a formal Kashmiri feast - a Wazwaan.

A Wazwan is a multi-course meal in the Kashmiri Muslim tradition. Its preparation is considered an art and is cooked by special cooks called 'waza's. It can have upto 36 preparations - seekh kabab, meth maaz, tabak maaz, barbecued ribs, safed kokur, and zafrani kokur, and what not. Not to mention salads, Kashmiri pickles and dips. Yum Yum.

It is like a foodie wet dream!

If any kind Kashmiri people read this, please do invite us to your next Wazwan.

After this huge feast, we ended with some excellent Kahwa - a Kashmiri green tea made with saffron, spices, almonds and walnuts and it was a perfect ending to a memorable meal.

We reluctantly squeezed ourselves into our riding gear, as we prepared to leave. It was a task to fit into it after such a huge meal.

We hit the road again immediately, as we did not want to risk getting stuck in some stupid curfew or the other. It was a frequent experience in Srinagar – some asshole terrorist would blow a bomb somewhere, and the whole town would go into lockdown. Its such a pity, because its is such a beautiful place and filled with all kinds of architecture, arts and craft, weaving, papier-mâché stuff and all kinds of culture, not to mention the amazing lakes and house boats and mughal gardens and stuff. But things seem to be simmering down over the years and one hopes for a peaceful Srinagar in times to come.

We fuelled up in Srinagar, as this would be the last metro city we would be seeing till Kargil and set out to Sonamarg. It was a nice ride but it was almost dark by the time we got to Sonamarg.

When we got there, I couldn't believe my eyes at the difference in Sonamarg from when I had visited ten years ago. At that time it was a tiny place with just one big hotel and a few tea shops. It was not a place to stay in at all – just a day trip from Srinagar and back, or a way station for those going on a short trek out there. I had stopped there enroute to Leh, and a firang couple had asked me where I was planning to stay. I thought I was being the cool backpacker dude when I said that I would stay in a cheap hotel costing about 300 rupees; but he had sneered at me and said that they were going to sleep on the floor of a local tea shop for 50 bucks! After taking the stand of a cool cheap traveller, I couldn't back out and had also joined them there and slept on the floor with them.

It was such a tiny place, with just a handful of shacks serving food and very heavy army presence – a young officer and his sergeant came around looking suspiciously at us, and you got the feeling that you were in a war zone, fully expecting to hear shots and explosions at any time.

Now the place was a bustling eyesore of a place, with hotels as far as the eye could reach. I stood there goggling in disbelief, as bawa and Adi came and impatiently honked.

'Here, relax' I said. 'Don't worry – we have reached out destination.'

'But let's check in…and enter a hotel.' Adi whined 'Or someone will shoot me.'

Bawa and me rolled our eyes.

'OK – let's check out the rates here'

We rode into the nearest hotel. It looked and smelt brand new; but it also looked expensive. I clucked my tongue doubtfully and went to speak with the manager. He looked absolutely delighted to see me – the hotel was so brand new, that we must have been his first guests.

He showed me his rooms and they were quite nice. Brand new and still smelling of paint and varnish, he was clearly aiming for the top end of tourist traffic.

'How much?', I enquired and he replied smilingly '4500 rupees'

'Fuck you too' I replied equally smilingly, and turned to get back on my bike; but the guy came running and stopped me with a hand on my elbow.

'Here...don't run away like that. You are my first guests of the season – I won't let you walk out just like that.'

'Season? What season?'

'The Amarnath yatra season, of course.'

Oho..now I got it – that's why there were so many hotels there. The government had opened another road to Amarnath from Sonmarg, so as to reduce the pressure on the Pahalgam route. This whole mess of hotels was to serve that demand.

'Shit!' I replied 'Are the Amarnath yatris coming today?' Indian tourist groups are a pain, but the religious tourist groups are the most painful of them all. They think that because they are out on a pious mission, any amount of noise and trash they make is OK. Nothing more dangerous than a bunch of idiots convinced of their own rightness.

'No no...' he assured me 'The groups will start in a day or two. But tell me – what is the problem? Why are you leaving?'

'No way I am paying 4500 bucks to stay here man.' I replied 'That is a ridiculous rate.'

'Ok...how much will you pay?'

'500 bucks for the 3 of us' I replied, and he gasped in disbelief.

A little bargaining happened, and we finally closed the deal at 1000 bucks for the 3 of us. Adi and bawa gave me respectful looks. Here is the master negotiator, they were thinking. He knows the correct value of the room and doesn't get cowed down by the asking price. This is the way to bargain! I paid him in advance, so that he wouldn't whine in the morning and we took possession of the room.

After changing, we came out and asked him where we can get some dinner.

'Here, of course' he replied 'I have a nice hotel as well...see?' he pointed at the sign.

I saw the sign 'Shuddh shakahai – Pure vegetarian'

'We are not interested in shudh shakahari man – we are not yatris. We want non vegetarian, which is obviously not available here.'

'Tchah!' he said dismissively. 'We put up that board just to keep the yatris happy. What would you like to have?'

'TANDOORI TANDOORI TANDOORI TANDOORI TANDOORI !' bawa yelled from behind. Inspite of eating the finest of Kashmiri food just a few hours ago, his lust for tandoori chicken was still unabated. Feed the bugger a five course French meal in the finest Michelin starred hotel in Paris, and he will still scream for tandoori. Even if goes to heaven when he dies (an unlikely occurence) , if they offer him nectar and ambrosia he will refuse and pine for tandoori chicken.

I cocked an enquiring eyebrow at the hotel chappie, and he said 'Not to worry sir! I will get you tandoori, never fear'

We sat down with another half of Old Monk, with bawa again trying to clean the stash of trash that he had brought, and Adi doing his imitation of a Saint Bernard waiting for scraps. Cleaning that was a monumental labour, ranking up there with Hercules cleaning the Augean stables.

After a while, the tandoori turned up, and man! It was simply amazing! Succulent, juicy, tasty, straight out of the oven – it was like a little piece of paradise in your mouth! We gobbled it up with gusto and immediately ordered another one!

I finished off the rum, and when the second bird arrived, it was even better than the first! We gobbled that one up too.

'Encore!' bawa said grandly. We looked at him.

'Dude, we have already had 2 birds.'

'So what? I normally have 2 birds on my own! Because I am biking I am on a diet, so I will have only one bird. Encore I say! Bring me another bird, or I shall start getting violent. I feel the need....the need to feed!!'

And so we had a third tandoori. I don't know whether it was the fatigue of the eater or the fatigue of the cook, but it was not to the same stratospheric level of the first two.

After we burped and belched and pissed mightily in the bushes, I thought that I might as well pay the bill now itself, so that we can make an early start tomorrow if required.

'How much?' I asked the hotel guy.

He smiled and replied '2700 rupees!'

'WTF!' I was shocked. All the rum vanished from my system and I was suddenly sober as a judge! '2700 bucks for a dinner!'

'Yes sir...600 bucks a piece for the chicken and the rest for soft drinks and stuff.'

'600 bucks for a chicken!' I clutched my forehead and reeled.

I paid and came back, and I thought that I could hear the hotel guy sniggering. The great bargainer indeed – he had got his money by hook or by crook – if not as room rent, then as hotel bill.

Ah well….the chicken had really been excellent, and the room was nice too.

Sonamarg to Portukchey

The next morning, I got the shock of my life, when the hotel owner himself came to the window and bellowed like a sergeant major 'UTHO REY! UTHO REY! UTHO! GET UP! GET UP! GET UP LAZYBONES!'

I sat upright in shock, my heart hammering.

'WTF dude?' I protested weakly.

'Terribly sorry sir..' the hotelier said, his features rigid with horror 'but I got a call from a Bharathi madam from Mumbai and she ordered me to wake you up with these words. I didn't dare to go against her orders.' He was still sweating and trembling from the phone call.

'WTF dude?' I protested 'How did she even know we were here?'

'Apparently she has been calling all hotels in Sonamarg to find out where you were sir...there is a pall of horror all over the valley. Three hoteliers have had heart attacks and one has gone insane with fear sir…please utho rey and go away sir…'

Soon we were ready - all eagle eyed and serious. This was where the ride was getting into the business end – we were going to leave the Kashmir valley and cross the first high pass – the famous Zojila pass. Zoji pass is quite a high pass of about 3500 meters, and it is snowed under for half the year. And this is inspite of the fact that it is a very important military asset for India because it is the only practical link between Ladakh and Kashmir, and the Border Roads Organisation is constantly trying to keep it clear with all the might of machines and men that they can bring to bear.

The pass had been closed during the night, either to allow movement of military convoys or maybe just to prevent drivers from falling off the mountain in the dark. It opened at first light and we were among the first civilians to go through. The hotelwala had been still trembling as we waved goodbye.

The pass was tough – steep and muddy – and I wondered at the expertise of the truck drivers who did this for a living. Adi's eyes nearly bugged out of his helmet when he saw a truck in front of him which had two of its tyres hanging in the air above a 1000 feet drop. Two trucks were crossing each other and there wasn't room for both of them. The guy on the mountain side obviously couldn't go any further into the mountain, so the guy on the valley side moved aside until a couple of his tyres were off the road and then depended on the traction of the remaining tyres to get him back on the road. Crazy stuff – but the driver seemed quite nonchalant. All in a day's work, as far as he was concerned.

In the olden days, it was only a trail, which you could only walk on. Even ponies couldn't pass it, and all merchandise was carried by porters. Not that there was much merchandise – mainly pashmina wool for the kashmiri carpet makers. But when Dogra General Zoravar Singh captured Ladakh in the 1830's, the road was improved – making it possible for pony wagons to pass.

Those were the days of the short lived Sikh Empire, when Ranjit Singh stepped into the power vacuum formed by the decline of the Mughal empire and the shock loss of the Maratha empire to the Afghans, and carved out a Sikh kingdom consisting of modern day Pakistan, parts of Afghanistan, and modern day North India.

But the Sikh empire crashed and burnt after the death of its founder, and within 10 years of Ranjit Singh's death, it had collapsed. T. Between those wars, the heirs fought violently amongst themselves and murdered each other, fought with the British and lost to them and in the blink of an historical eye, the British empire was in control of the entire Sikh Empire.

But those were the days of the first cold war - 'The great game' as Rudyard Kipling called it, where the Russian Empire and the British empire were facing off. The British were very afraid that the Russians would send an army across the land route of Russia, Central Asia and Afghanistan to invade India and chuck out the British. For that reason, they wanted a local buffer state and so allowed both Afghanistan and Kashmir to remain as independent states. They sold Kashmir to the King of Jammu and tasked him with building a decent road and keeping the Zoji la pass in good repair - good enough for troops to pass though if necessary. This was the first time that Zojila was made military ready in the modern sense.

The next repair of the road happened after the Pakistani wars and then after the Chinese aggression, when we found out too late that the chinks had built excellent all weather roads into Ladakh. Actually we found that out after China built a road into Aksai Chin, stole the area, thumbed their nose at us and then thumped us when we tried to object.

So basically it takes a war to get the government to maintain roads. Then the only hope for Bombay to get good roads is to start a war there.

The BRO keeps trying to keep the pass in good repair, but it is pretty tough. The roads get covered in snow every winter, with drifts of upto 60 feet – and when they carve the ice open with snow ploughs, it scrapes off any tarmac with it, leaving just a muddy scar which they call a road. I was admiring the BRO for keeping the road open.

Bharathi immediately sneered at me inside my head, using patented nag technology 'OTHER COUNTRIES ALSO HAVE SNOW – HOW DO THEY KEEP THEIR ROADS OPEN? HAH!' but with an effort I pushed her out of my head.

The Pakistan Rangers had actually captured this pass in the 1947 war in their attempt to take over Ladakh, but it was retaken by Indian forces in a daring assault codenamed Operation Bison– they brought tanks over here! In 1947! In November ! Even in peak summer, in 2013, it would be tough to bring tanks here – they did it in winter, under gunfire, back then when the road must have been much worse even to reach the pass. Those guys must have had balls as big as water melons.

We crossed the enigmatically named 'Captain mod' – where some said that a Captain had fallen to his death during road construction, while others say that the said Captain committed suicide for some reason or the other, while a third account is that he drove off the cliff intentionally with his wife and children in the jeep – no doubt after having been charged Rs 600 per chicken for dinner.

I was grimly riding on, wondering when the hard part would come, when I suddenly felt a strange feeling under the wheel. When I stopped to check, I found that it was tarmac!

Arre! Ye kya? Tarmac in the middle of Zojila pass? What miracle is this? I looked around and saw that the mountains were only behind me – not in front of me. The pass was over. We were in Ladakh now.

Well – that was easier than I thought. Barely broke a sweat in Zojila.

I saw a tent near the mountain and we went to check it out. It turned out to be a pit stop place serving tea and snacks and we responded in various individual ways.

'TEA!' I said. 'HOT TEA! YIPEE!"

'MAGGI!' Adi screamed, probably orgasming in his pants. He never outgrew his childish passion for Maggi, and I think his main attraction of coming on this ride was because he had heard that you get only Maggi to eat over here. He got off his bike and started singing and dancing 'MAGGI MAGGI MAGGI...'

'MOUNTAIN! ICE! SNOW! BAD ROADS! ROCKS! SLUDGE!' screamed Bawa and rushed off up the mountain and into the snow. He had been fantasising about off-roading and riding on the worst roads possible. He had been dreaming of ice and rocks and rabid rivers and impassable mud, and was probably deeply disappointed by the ease of Zojila, and so when he saw snow so close by, he couldn't control himself.

He zoomed off, and Adi couldn't bear to stay still when he could be moving, so he zoomed off after him.

'Damn and blast' I muttered under my breath and trundled along after them. I would much rather have had a cup of tea and soak in the beauty of the place rather than fool about riding in the snow. But I couldn't stay behind and be exposed as a wimp, could I? So, I also went up and soon we were all parked halfway up the mountain parked in the middle of a snow bank. After taking a few photos and throwing snow at each other, it was time to go down. I looked at the descent doubtfully – it's always easier to climb up than to go down – you don't need to use your brake while climbing, as you can control your speed just by leaving your throttle and downshifting your gear. While going down you have to depend on your brake, as you can pick up surprising speed even in bottom gear, and that can cause you to slip and fall.

'Don't worry' Bawa grandly told me 'Do (blablabla advice blablabla) and you will be fine' So I went down slowly and nervously and soon I was down by the tent and ordering tea. Adi came bouncing down and was ordering Maggi. Maggi Maggi Maggi.

We looked up at the mountain, and Bawa was on the floor!

'AAAARGHHHH!' Adi screamed, like a heroine keening for her demon lover 'DELZAD HAS FALLEN!! EEEK!!' and without even thinking, he started running up the mountain towards the fallen bawa.

I just stood there and demanded my tea.

'You are not going to see your friend?' the chaiwala enquired, without too much interest.

'Nah.' I saw that Bawa was up already, and was picking up his bike. He had just slipped a bit. 'He is fine. I am just worried about that fool who is running up.' And indeed Adi's speed had slowed drastically and I could hear him huffing and puffing from here. 'WAIT ...BAWA...I AM...huff...COMING...puff...I ...am....huffpuffhuffpuff...cooommm....'. 'I hope he doesn't have a heart attack or something.'

Bawa got his bike up with the help of a local and came bouncing down with an embarrassed look on his face. 'I slipped a little and lost control of the bike.' He explained 'So I stepped away and let the bike fall.' He looked around 'Where's Adi?'

I pointed to the mountain, and Del swivelled to look and saw a very angry and out of breath Adi at the place where Del had fallen - looking at us and spreading his hands in disgust.

'What's he doing up there?' Delzad asked in puzzlement, as Adi started his long walk down.

The scenery on this side of Zojila was completely different from the Kashmir side. The Kashmir side was green and lush, while the Ladakh side was brown and sere. The sky was a deep azure blue and dotted with white clouds – and the land was brown and red and all kinds of earth colour shades. the whole scene was just a palette of gods colours – it was amazing.

It was so beautiful that it was a real task to keep your eyes on the road.

And no doubt that it was for this reason that the BRO decided to keep the road in such bad repair. It forced you to concentrate on the road so as to avoid the stones and craters in the road. The road would be made on the left side for some time, and then abruptly that would be under construction and you would have to go to the other side.

So here we were, concentrating on the road, negotiating some seriously bad stretches , when I got the scare of my life while going down a steep slope.

My brake failed! On a steep slope! WTF!

My life flashed before my eyes, as I desperately jammed on my rear brake and it wouldn't respond at all. I zoomed past the surprised others on the slope and managed to stay upright and stop by downshifting and jamming on my front brake. The bike fishtailed a bit (swerved from side to side like a fish's tail wagging) but stood upright.

The two Amigos stopped and I explained the problem. Bawa's eyes lit up! This was the moment he had been waiting for! A breakdown! Some reason to use the array of tools that he had been carting around. He rubbed his hands with glee and opened his tool bag.

'Let's see now....your brake pad may have got damaged...or maybe your hydraulics are gone...maybe the brake oil has leaked out – in which case you are truly fucked, because that's the one thing we are not carrying...' he opened the cap of the brake oil reservoir and grunted with disappointment when he saw it was all fine. 'Maybe the disks are damaged...maybe the saddlebag is impeding the brake...'

He kept muttering to himself as he burrowed deeper and deeper into the bike, and his hair seemed to pulse with his heartbeat as he got more frustrated. I was getting nervous, thinking about how to get the bike to a repairman in case bawa couldn't figure it out.

Adi and bawa were crawling all over the bike and finally bawa said 'Eureka!'

Well, he didn't say 'Eureka' – what he said was 'MADARCHOT!'

He found the problem, and it was a problem that only a Royal Enfield could have, because the quality control of Royal Enfield sucks ass. The exhaust pipe, which lets out the burnt gas from the engine, can get very hot because the gas has just come out of the engine after the petrol has been burnt. So, as a safety measure, Royal Enfield has attached a heat shield - a small metal plate on top of the exhaust outlet where the rider would be keeping his foot. This, they smugly point out, is a wonderful thing that they do, as it would prevent the rider from getting a nasty burn and cursing aloud if he is silly enough to put his foot on the exhaust. Then they high-five each other and go and raise the cost of the bike by ten thousand bucks.

Unfortunately, they attach that stupid little plate with the cheapest screws they can find, so when the bike vibrates while riding the screws become loose, and that protective plate is not held tightly, and it falls upside down due its own weight. And then...follow me closely here...that fuck-all little plate is perfectly designed to fit just below the brake lever and blocks it and prevents it from being pressed! So now you have a 200 kg motorcycle which does not have a rear brake.

Recently Royal Enfield proudly announced that they sold more bikes than Harley Davidson worldwide – which news one should take with a pinch of salt as it costs only a fraction of a hog. By that logic, Bajaj and Hero Honda would be sniggering into their sideburns and winking at each other.

Another more concrete news is that the share price of Eicher motors has gone from from 17 bucks to 15000 bucks in 15 years. Thats crazy stuff. The market awards that kind of valuation rarely.

That's the kind of value that the company enjoys – in a large part due to Royal Enfield bikes. The sales have skyrocketed – an RE was a rarity even when I got into biking 5 years back – now every Tom, Deepak and Hari seem to have one. The cost of the bike has gone from 55000 in 2001 to 2,00,000 today, but still they are flying off the shelves. They spend almost nothing on advertising and promotion – why should they, when they have waiting periods more than 6 months long for the bike?

Siddharth Lal has worked a modern day miracle with Royal Enfield.

And it must have made him very rich indeed – just on his share holdings alone, quite apart from the huge profits of the running business.

So my question to Sid Lal is – why is your quality so fucking horrible? Not one RE fresh out of the factory can be said to have unimpeachable quality. To put it bluntly – RE quality sucks.

I love my Royal Enfield – as do the entire community of riders around the nation. That's why we still stick to the bike and coddle it through every illness that it gets. We pay premium prices for the bikes, but every part of it breaks down and then we get ripped off by the service stations. We love it and yet we get fucked by RE. Why?

Possibly we are a community of masochists and Sid Lal is the Christian Grey of biking.

Thats a good name for the bike – 500 cc's of grey!

Chalo - rant over.

Delzad tore the heat shield off, and voila – the brake was fine!

I cursed RE, its makers and its quality control department at great length and we continued on to Drass. Drass is supposed to be the second coldest inhabited place on earth – after the Siberian village of Oymyakon - wherever that is. But it is in a nice valley, with a nice river – the Drass river - running through it and we could see lovely flowers and stuff as we rode through.

It is supposed to be inhabited by a community of people very different than the rest of the Ladakhis - they are called Dards, and they are supposed to be descendants of some vague Aryan tribes from central Asia, and speak some language of their own called Shina. The interesting thing is that they are muslims – unlike the mostly Buddhist Ladakhis.

The place is also the venue of the Kargil war memorial, erected by the Indian Army. It's a largish complex, with various buildings having photos and land models and information about the Kargil war, where the Pakistani irregulars attacked that sensitive area and managed to give us quite a bloody nose before getting killed off.

From Drass, we went on to Kargil town, which is the midpoint of the Sonamarg-Leh route. It was a very pleasant ride – bright sun, cool breeze, blue sky, white cottony clouds and the scenery was pretty nice too. There's plenty of water due to the rivers, and so there is a good bit of farming and stuff.

The Kargil route has been a part of the historic mercantile route since history, so Kargil was always an important stopping town on the way to Leh. So the town is pretty ancient and apparently has a couple of ancient mosques and atmospheric bazaars and shit – which, needless to say, we didn't bother to see. Even when travelling by myself, imambaras and bazaars are not on the top of my must-see things in life, and when we were travelling with Mr Perpetual Motion himself... well, they never had a chance. Left to himself, Kargil would just have been a blur on the road, but we caught him by the collar (metaphorically) and forced him to stop for lunch.

We stopped at a nondescript hotel and we pleasantly surprised to see Kashmiri food on the menu. Well, Adi was disappointed – he wanted Maggi; but me and Delzad were happy. Even bad Kashmiri food is good food.

We had just finished our meal, and were sitting and digesting, and wondering if we should stay the night in Kargil or push on for Leh, when I saw the waiter come towards us. I looked at him carefully – he was white faced and trembling, and walking with a peculiar stiff gait.

'Uh oh' I said – surely not.... 'Did you get a phone call, by any chance...?'

'UTHO REY! UTHO REY! UTHO! GET UP YOU LAZY SWABS! AVAST! STOP EATING SO MUCH AND RIDE!' he bellowed so loudly that Adi slipped and fell back on the chair which cracked and broke beneath his weight. Bawa just continued eating his meat balls.

'RIDE TO ZANSKAR VALLEY! TAKE THE TURNOFF FROM KARGIL TO PADUM!'

'But...we were planning to go to Leh...' I protested weakly

'GO TO PADUM YOU MORON! WHEN WILL YOU GET A CHANCE TO GO TO ZANSKAR AGAIN?'

'But...we were planning to go to Lahul Spiti...' I still protested

'HOW DARE YOU ARGUE WITH THE TRAVEL GURU, YOU IGNORANT BUMPKIN?!!' the waiter screamed even louder, a couple of glasses shattering at his voice, as the veins in his throat swelled and his eyes popped. 'YOU WILL BE ABLE TO GO TO SPITI ANYTIME, BUT YOU WILL NEVER GO TO ZANSKAR AGAIN. SO STOP ARGUING AND MOVE! MOVE! MOVE! UTHO REY! UTHO!'

The waiter collapsed as his mental connection to Bharathi was severed and we rushed out of the hotel and ran for our bikes, and we were on our way to Zanskar, leaving the Leh road behind.

Kargil is a junction point – with a road going towards Leh, and one road going southwards towards the Zanskar region. The main town there was Padum, and we were planning on going there. I personally had no idea about the place whatsoever. I had heard the name a couple of times, but that was about the Chadar trek – when the Zanskar river freezes solid in the winter and forms a solid sheet of ice. The locals think that this is a better road to climb that area instead of the rocky mountain paths, something which says a lot about the place...and about the locals.

But that was the extent of my knowledge. The other two had no idea at all – they were not even sure of the spelling. But they were happy – Adi was happy because it was a road and he could keep riding ROADS! WOO HOO! , and Delzad was happy because someone said that it might be in bad condition, and the idea of off roading was balm to his soul. BAD ROADS. WOO HOO.

We went happily down the road to Padum, and it was great fun – it was a nice new smooth road with a lot of curves, so we were happily zooming away on the road and enjoying bending on the turns and enjoying the scenery.

At one point, I was riding in front of the group and there was a white van in front of me driving right in the middle and hogging the road. It was frustrating to be tailing a vehicle on such an empty road and I got irritated with the slow speed of the van and decided to overtake it once the turn got over – I have this rule of never overtaking unless I can see the road in front of me. As the road opened, I gave her the throttle and overtook the van, and while overtaking it I noticed that it was actually an ambulance.

For a split second, I was admiring the ubiquity of the Maruti Omni – after it tanked as a passenger vehicle, Maruti almost withdrew it from the market, until some sharp eyed fellow noticed that there was a brisk market for second hand Omnis. When they investigated it, they found that the simple bread box design of the vehicle was very amenable to storage, so people were ripping out all the seats and making it into a cheap and manoeuvrable luggage carrier. Maruti also liked the idea and relaunched the Omni as a cheap and affordable people and luggage carrier. So now Omnis are delivery vans, school buses, road side restaurants – and ambulances!

But only for a split second! Just as I overtook the van, I saw that there was a humongous speed breaker right in front of me, just at the overtaking point. With absolutely no way to brake, I went DHADAAM into the speed breaker and was thrown into the air, I became airborne like Evel Knievel doing a stunt over a row of trucks or something. My bike was in the air, my ass was in the air – luckily my hands didn't come off the handlebar!

The only thought I had at the time apart from 'OH SHIIIIIITTTT!' was 'Luckily there's an ambulance behind me – if I fall and break my bones, the ambulance can help out.'

Luckily I didn't need the ambulance – the Thunderbird 500 is so well designed that it landed squarely back on both wheels with hardly a wobble, and I also landed DHUPPP on the seat and was back, both literally and figuratively, on the saddle.

My heart pounding, I slowed down and let the ambulance pass me. I could just imagine the driver tapping his forehead and saying 'these bikers are crazy'.

It was evening by then, and after some time, we took a smart turn on the highway and stopped in consternation! The highway had vanished! The beautiful tarmac road we were on had suddenly vanished! There was no road of any kind.

Puzzled, we stopped the bikes and looked around. How strange. What has happened? Did we take a wrong turn somewhere? But how was that possible....there had been no turn at all on the road.

We looked at each other and shrugged. This was like Tolkein stuff – the invisible gates of Moria. There should be a couple of gates here which I can hammer against and say the elvish word for friend - 'Mellon', and the gates would magically appear and open.

With these two, if I said 'Mellon' they would think I am asking for fruit. Or boobs. Big boobs.

Anyway, there we were waiting in the darkling eve – when we heard a roar of an approaching vehicle. I thought that it might be a truck or a JCB or some construction vehicle bravely making a road in the trackless waste. We could stop him and ask him the directions to civilisation, because we were clearly lost in some uncharted path.

What came out of the gloom was a ....schoolbus full of children! One....Two....three...Four schoolbuses....with banners on them....it was a primary school picnic!

Good heavens. That rocky muddy track which we thought was a cow track or something was actually the national highway!

We set out on that national highway in a cloud of dust. As the evening became darker, I was getting more and more uncomfortable – not wanting to be on this road in the dark.

Luckily, we saw a J&K tourism bungalow at a village called Portukchey and went there to investigate. Sometimes you can stay in these places without a reservation and sometimes they insist on a reservation to be done beforehand. But luckily there was no hassle out here, which was a relief. The decayed old Gorkha caretaker didn't have a room, but he had dorm beds. That was absolutely fine with us. In fact we turned out to be the only people in the dorm, so it was as if we had got the biggest room in the house for the a throwaway price. It was a lovely little property – with a little garden in front and a nice view of the Nun and Kun mountains. The caretaker explained that this bungalow was a stopping point for people who went on mountaineering expeditions to Nun and Kun.

We ordered some food – I knew the type of the caretaker and estimated that he had maybe an hour of sobriety left. As soon as the sun came down, the bottle will be out. Better get everything done before he gets smashed for the night. We got the food, but forgot to tell him to lay out the bedding. But that was OK – we had sleeping bags with us and this was a chance to use them.

The dorm was on the first floor and we had a lovely view of the Nun and Run mountains from the window there.

I slept nicely that night – it had been a longish day, and we had crossed the mighty Zoji La without any mishaps.

Portukchey to Padum

'CAW CAW'

'CAW CAW'

'CAW CAW'

'CAW CAW!!!!!!!!!'

I was woken up by the incessant, insistent and indignant nagging of the crow at the window sill. It was a Himalayan raven – big, jet black and definitely angry looking. It looked like a witch's familiar. It glared at me through its beady black eyes and again shouted 'CAW CAW'

'Hud. Hisht. Shoo.' I said and threw a sock at it, but it wouldn't move. It seemed to get even angrier and said 'CAW CAW CAW....UTHO REY....CAW CAW....UTHO REY....CAW CAW....UTHO REY!'

I sat up upright with a jerk. I should have known. Everything was familiar – the colour, the expression, the sound...

'UTHO REY! GET MOVING! YOU HAVE TO CROSS RANGDUM MONASTERY AND PENSI LA AND GET TO PADUM BEFORE DARK!'

'Penis La?' Even in my sleepy state, that sounded weird.

'PENSI LA!'

'Pansy La?' Was it so easy that the other passes laughed at it and called it a pansy?

'PEN - SI .....CAW.....LA!'

'Oh...Pensi la. What about it?'

'ITS A BLOODY HIGH PASS! YOU HAVE TO PASS THAT TO GET TO PADUM! AND LOOK AT YOUR PANSY FRIENDS! THEY HAVE ALREADY GOT ALTITUDE SICKNESS! CAW CAW'

'Eh?' I turned and saw both those moron clutching their heads and moaning ....OOOOOHhhh... If not for the crow's statement, I would have thought that both had sneaked into the liquor stocks last night and got a hangover.

Altitude sickness is caused by lack of oxygen in the air, and can get nasty. In its mild form itself it is quite unpleasant – making you feel all sick and pukey and headachey and hangovery – A hangover without alcohol is like going to hell without even enjoying the sin. At its more nasty end it can cause swellings in the lungs and brain and can kill.

I turned to the raven and asked 'So what do I do now?'

'I HAVE ALREADY PACKED DIAMOX IN YOUR MEDICAL KIT – NOW SHUT UP AND GIVE THEM A PILL AND GET GOING!!! UTHO!! CAW CAW CAW CAW CAW CAW'

Such was the power of that last Caw, that the three of us were packed and geared and on our bikes in record time.

The road was breathtaking. Fantastic vistas on both sides, and no traffic on the road. Forget traffic, there was hardly any human habitation to be seen.

This area can really be said to be the last frontier of India. A land where one can walk for miles without coming across any human habitation. A land of unspoilt valleys, of harsh and forbidding mountains and deep blue skies.

The road was a kaccha road, without any tarmac visible. The government had obviously laid a tarmac road once – you could see remains of it here and there – but harsh ice and snow in winters had erased every sign of it. It was like discovering an ancient roman road or perhaps the mysterious road that Allan Quatermain and his companions found in 'King Solomon's mines' – an ancient and forgotten path laid out eons ago by a great but long forgotten civilisation.

According to the Collins guide, this area is known as the 'Land of white copper'. This made me give a mental head slap – 'White copper?' always thought that copper is .....well....coppery. brownish golden kind of colour.

'Zanskar' itself gets its name from 'Zangs dkar' which means white copper (!) - a reference to the copper deposits in the region. Its a huge 5000 square kilomter area between the Zanskar and the Great Himalayan ranges, and consists of the valleys of the Stod and the Tsarup rivers, which merge at Padum to form the Zanskar valley.

Earlier the only way to reach this place was by foot – Now we have this road that we were riding on – once metalled, now a dirt track. This road is passable only for four months of summer. Thus the beauty and mystery of this place was still maintained to some extent.

This is really the land to come to for a tryst with the past, for a trip into the unknown – a trip that would test both bike and biker.

ARRE, I CAME TO THIS PLACE WHEN YOU WERE STILL PISSING IN YOUR PANTS !

I almost fell off my bike in panic. Now she was channelling straight into my brain.

I CAME HERE WHEN NO ONE HAD EVEN HEARD THE NAME.

EVEN THE MAP MAKER HAD TO ASK ME THE SPELLING.

THERE WAS NO ROAD AT THAT TIME. ONLY A DONKEY COULD TRAVERSE THE PATH.

SOMETIMES THE ROAD WAS SO BAD, I HAD TO CARRY THE DONKEY ON MY SHOULDERS.

AND YOU ARE COMPLAINING ABOUT THE CONDITION OF THE ROAD....

The connection suddenly broke when a particularly bad patch of road nearly threw me off. I was riding along grimly, when I heard a WOO HOOO and saw Bawa speeding along with a big grin on his face! He was deliberately choosing the worst patches of the road and enjoying himself on the bumps and grinds, like some demented springbok jumping around on the veldt. He spent more time in the air than on the ground.

Adi was spurred by this and he also got into the act and both were gone in the horizon in a cloud of dust, leaving me all alone in the coppery landscape.

I didn't even attempt to match their speed, but trundled along at my own happy pace, looking at the Marmots running around on the mountainside.

We crossed Parkachik, which was the place that we were planning to reach last night. It is an amazing quartet of glacier, mountain pass, ridge and village – all called Parkachik. Parkachik is the village on Parkachik ridge, which is topped by the 3810 meter high mountain pass of Parkachik La, which affords a fine view of Parkachik glacier.

So if you ask – 'have we reached Parkachik?' – all answers – Yes, No, Maybe – are valid.

I felt quite at home - in Mumbai, you arrive by train at Chattrapati Shivaji Terminus, you fly out from Chattrapati Shivaji Airport, you go to Chattrapati Shivaji Museum, etc etc - so this same name for everything was familiar to me.

By noon we came to the village of Juldo, which was just a small collection of huts. The main virtue of this place was that it was the attendant village of the Rangdum Monastery, and it was the only stopping point on the way to Padum, where one could have a bite of food.

There was a firang biker there, with an ancient Royal Enfield. He had bought the bike second hand in Delhi, and had planned to ride all around India on it.
But he was having a problem with his bike - it was overheating and losing power. Being a tinkerer kind of guy, he had tried to fix it himself. He had taken it apart and find out the issue and had discovered that his crank case was leaking! This was a very big deal because the crank case houses the bath of engine oil which lubricates

and cools the moving parts of the engine. Without engine oil, the whole engine would heat and seize up and die in minutes. He had isolated the problem and was now wondering how to plug the leak. The only way to do this would be to take it to a workshop and weld the leak - but where to find those here in the mountains?

Bawa felt sorry for him, , and gave him some M-seal to patch his leak. But that was a very long shot, and unlikely to work for long.

I shuddered at the thought of being a solo rider with a dickey bike in Zanskar, but he seemed to be cool with it. He was a repair nerd like Bawa, and they spent some time chatting about the disembowelled bike - how they could adjust the doohickey by schtupping the thingamajig and tronking the whatsit... Both of them enjoyed the conversation hugely, like two doctors pondering over a terminal patient.

It seemed to me that a truck ride was in this bike's future. In a sack.

We could see the Rangdum monastery in the distance, on top of a little hill. Its more than 200 years old, and apparently is famous for having a lot of donkeys – as many donkeys as monks. No, I don't know what they do with so many donkeys.

Since we weren't carrying any food of any sort, we were very relieved to find a place to eat. And as one might expect in such a wild landscape, it wasn't exactly cordon bleu cuisine available there.

You had a choice between rice rajma and rajma rice.

'We will have the rajma rice' I said with dignity.

'An excellent choice sir' the waiter clicked his pen with approval and went off, and was soon back with 3 plates of gloopy stuff, looking more like his turds than rajma.

I looked down at it doubtfully, and as I raised my head, I saw Bawa licking the last grains of rice off his plate! He had gobbled it down faster than a frog scarfing down a fly!

'What?' he said, as both of us stared at him in disbelief 'I was hungry.'

I just pushed the stuff around on my plate, and it seemed to push right back. Just as I was looking at it, and wondering whether to force myself to eat it, a guide came over to chat and quietly warned me not to eat it. 'God knows when it was made' he said 'be careful'

That was enough for me – I left it mostly uneaten, and filled up with some biscuits and soft drinks instead.

'Arre, kuch nahin hota re...' Bawa started off confidently 'Eat it. It's all good! Only wimps are scared to ....ooof' he stopped suddenly and rubbed his tummy 'scared to eat......burp burrrrrp' his eyes widened in panic as he thought of the long road ahead.

'Oh boy' I said to Adi 'He is really going to enjoy the ride today'
'Yeah..' Adi agreed. 'He is going to love that bumpy road'
'What nonsense are you guys talking? It was an excellent plate of rajmaaaaaaaaaah' he exclaimed as his belly twisted inside him, and he valiantly repressed a huge fart, which came out as a timid 'tweep' instead.
'It's gonna be a rocket propelled ride.' I remarked, as he ran for his bike.

We passed a group of utterly exhausted looking bikers returning from Padum, as we totally raced past Rangdum monastery.
'Hey!' I shouted 'Where are you guys rushing off to? Don't you want to see the monastery? The Monks? The Donkeys?' But all I could see was the dust. I sighed and went off after them.

OY. WHY AREN'T YOU GOING TO RANGDUM?

I STAYED THERE BEFORE ELECTRICITY CAME TO THIS REGION.

I TAUGHT THE HEAD MONK TO MAKE IDLI AND CHUTNEY…

I TAUGHT THE ACOLYTES TO WEAR LUNGIS…

But alas, I had to ignore her, as I raced along after them. Bawa was on fire – he just zoomed past the scenery, barely seeming to touch the ground, leaving behind smells of burnt rubber and dirty farts.

We came to a stream of meltwater from the snowcapped mountains – as the sun had come out, more and more snow had melted and swelled the stream from a gentle brook to a raging torrent. A pair of Spanish bicyclists were stranded glumly on one side of it – it was too big for them to pass, so they would have to camp there overnight and cross the next morning when the snow had frozen again and the stream gone back to brook levels.

It didn't delay bawa for even a second though – he just put his feet on leg guards and zoomed through the stream with a roar. Adi couldn't hang back after that, and he too went through, beard jutting aggressively.

The Spaniards were impressed. 'Big bike, eh? Powerful.' One said. 'Ole!' exclaimed the other 'Arribba! Hombre!'

'Um...yeah. sure.' I muttered, and steeling myself, I went through the stream myself, splashing through the freezing water.

Pensi La was only 25 km from Rangdum. Its even higher than Zoji La – 4,400 meters vs 3528 meters – and its higher than any pass on the Srinagar Leh road. Its the gateway to the Zanskar region – till now we were in the Suru valley, and by crossing this pass, we were entering the Zanskar region. Thus it is the only road to Padum as of now. Due to its height, it is open only for 3-4 months in the summer.

It was a really beautiful sight at the pass. We could see the snowcapped ranges of the Zanskar range and the peaks of Nun and Kun, and the imposing Darang Durung glacier in the distance. Just the name itself was charming – Darang Durung.

There were also a couple of beautiful mountain lakes right on the top. We stopped there for some photos, until bawa zoomed off again as if his ass was on fire.

I wanted to enjoy the beauty of Darang Durung, so I went down sedately down the steep and curving road, enjoying the ride immensely.

As I reached the bottom, I saw both bikes standing and both riders lying on the ground!

'Oy – what happened? Did you have an accident?' I asked in panic.

'I nearly had an accident, but it was contained.' Delzad answered wearily.

'Good heavens! What happened?' I exclaimed.

'He had an explosion.' Adi sniggered.

'An explosion!' I was shocked. 'Where?'
'In his pants.'
'What?'
'Yeah man...' Delzad groaned. 'That rajma rice screwed me. I managed to make it down the mountain, but there was no cover in sight anywhere! There's no tree, no bush, no rock, no fold in the land – nothing! Where was I supposed to go to shit? Then finally I saw this rock way up the mountain and I just dumped my bike and ran for it.'
'I reached there and saw the bike and no Delzad. He had just vanished! I waited for some time and then finally he limps down the mountain complaining about his handkerchief.'
'Handkerchief?' that seemed an odd thing to complain about.
'Yeah man....I was so happy after a virtuous crap...but then I realised that I had no water to wash, and nothing to wipe with. There wasn't even a tree leaf or handful of grass, or even a flat rock to wipe with! So.....'
'But...your hanky!'
'Yeah man...it was a nice hanky...it had my name on it.'
'And now it has your bum on it.' We laughed loudly to assuage his feelings.

After two minutes silence in memory of his departed hanky, we continued on the way to Padum.
The road went on and on, in its dirt track glory, and I was starting to get anxious, looking at the setting sun. How long was this road, and how bad did it get before our destination?
The road itself was unmetalled, dirt road – which was not so bad – the bikes could do it. The bigger issue was the water crossings. The full day of sunlight had melted the snow in the mountains and the resulting meltwater was swelling the streams.

We had already crossed one biggish stream earlier, but when we came to the next one, we all stopped and gazed at it thoughtfully.

Hmmm.

The bloody thing was a river – not a stream. It flowed not with a mischievous gurgle, but with a scary throaty roar, bulging with the power of the mountain snow. You could have produced enough electricity to power all of Padum through that thing. 'Roaring torrent' , 'Raging cataract', 'ferocious rapids' were the words that ran through my head.

And there was no one around for miles. We were the only people in that landscape.

Hmmm.

Well, there was no choice really – we had to get to the other side of that water. Bawa just shrugged his shoulders and said 'I will go first.'
We tripped all over ourselves with politeness to allow him to go first. We did not wish to push and shove – oh no! We were most willing to let others have the first crack.

He put his bike in gear, and roared into the water! The current was so strong that it pushed his bike forward about 6 feet, and in the middle of the river, his bike stopped! Shit! The water was quite deep – came up to cover the tyre and looked quite forbidding. And about 10 feet away there was a steep drop where the water fell below in a scenic and noisy waterfall!
Pushing it was simply not an option, so he gritted his teeth and pressed the self start, hoping desperately that it would not fry his

electricals – and the engine started! With a sigh of relief, he managed to get his bike across the river and hauled it up the bank, dripping and steaming.

'Ketan – cross from this point...' he shouted, pointing at a spot. 'And be careful with the gear – don't let the engine cut.'
I gulped. I cleared my throat. I gathered my courage. I started my bike.
And rushed into the water! The water was fucking freezing! Just a degree away from being ice! My lower parts started shrieking! The force of the stream started pushing me towards the waterfall, and the tyres tried valiantly to get a grip on the slippery stones of the river bed.
And the engine died!
Shit, Shit, shit. I tried the self start, and it worked! The engine roared to life and I managed to cross the river and emerged on the other side, puffing and panting with the effort. The bike seemed to be fine, but I was bloody soaked in the freezing water.
I parked the bike and sat at the side of the path, gasping.

Next was Adi. He girded his loins and rushed into the water. And stopped. Unlike both of us, his engine did not cut. It was still roaring away, but he was not moving. He pushed and pulled desperately with his body, trying to get his bike to move, but to no avail. He was stuck in the fast moving freezing water, being pushed towards the waterfall.

And then suddenly, like genii materialising out of thin air, two locals appeared on the scene!

They took one look and without a word being spoken, jumped into the icy water to help us out. Delzad also jumped into the water. Two guys were pushing from behind, and one guy was pulling the handlebar, and Adi was desperately twisting the accelerator, causing the bike to roar in protest, but the bike was not moving.

At first, I thought that I would not be required to enter that water, but seeing that his bike was not moving, I sighed and entered the torrent to help out. AARRRGHH, my epidermis screamed as the cold hit me again.

Delzad was screaming at Adi – 'Release the clutch, you will burn out your clutch plate. You will strip your gear. Release your clutch!!!!'

Adi took his hand off the clutch completely to show that the clutch was indeed released. One of the locals slapped his hand aside contemptuously and twisted the accelerator savagely himself, causing both –the bike and Adi - to squeal in agony!

Still no avail! The bike wouldn't move!

What the fuck! What do we do now?

Then suddenly Delzad's expression turned from concern to outrage! His face went from being blue with cold, and gray with worry to being red with anger.

'YOU STUPID BLOODY ASSHOLE! THE NEUTRAL LIGHT IS ON!'

'Eh? What?' Adi said

'THE BIKE IS IN NEUTRAL, YOU IDIOT! PUT IT IN FIRST GEAR!'

Adi looked at him in disbelief, and engaged first gear.

And the bike smoothly moved out of the stream and out onto the bank, leaving the four of us in the water.

Delzad was so pissed, that I thought he was going to explode. His hair was curling and uncurling with emotion, like the fretful porpentine.

'WHAT KIND OF IDIOT DOESN'T REALISE THAT HIS BIKE IS NOT IN GEAR?' FOOL. DOG. PIG. BUFFOON.'
Adi was completely embarrassed. He went all red, and muttered something about false neutrals and faulty neutral lights and then shut up. He knew that we were not going to let him forget about this ever. Great. On the plus side, we were all across. On the minus side, we were soaked and freezing.

We thanked the locals, and the kind fate that sent two men there in the most desolate and unpopulated of all areas at the exact moment that we needed help.
They said that they were from a neighbouring village, and invited us to stay there overnight if we were tired, as Padum was still some distance away.
'No charge, free. Stay as our guest.' He said, and Adi and Delzad went pale.
Just the earlier night, I had been telling them about the cannibal of Mulbek. Apparently, at the village of Bodhkharbu, near Mulbek, on the Kargil Leh road; there was a singe hut that stood all by itself – inhabited by a cannibal! He would lure passers by with friendliness and a promise of hospitality and invite them to stay the night. And if they accepted, he would kill them in the night and eat them! This was in the 70's, and the man had since been arrested and jailed; but who knows how many others decided to follow his philosophy?
'No no...no thanks' we said to the helpful man, we wanted to get to Padum.
The guys were so nice, they refused to take even a paisa for helping us out.
'How far is Padum from here?' we asked. 50 km, they replied.
We sighed. That would mean an hour and a half, or two hours on this road.

We went on and on – and paled, as we came to yet another water crossing!

'SHIT' Delzad said, as he prepared to cross the water, and glared at Adi. 'Ensure your bike is in gear bugger!'

Adi must have stood on the gear lever this time, and we all staggered to the other side, soaked for the second time.

After an hour we came to a village, and for a moment, I hoped against hope that we had reached Padum – but no...it was some other place.

'How far is Padum from here?' we asked wearily. 'Not far...just 50 kilometers.'

WHAT? An hour ago, that fellow had said 50 km! Shit.

We carried on, and suddenly the road vanished! There was only a mountain side! It was as if someone had played a practical joke and laid out a path to a dead end.

Maybe some Ladakhi was leering down at us and shouting 'Chutiya banaya...bada maja aaya!' at that very moment.

We dismounted and stood there, as Pink Floyd would say 'Waiting for someone or something to show us the way!'

And luckily there was a truck coming up behind us. We knew that because we had arrogantly overtaken it with loud horns sometime back. Now we stood there quietly, waiting for it to come up.

We flagged him down and asked him about the mysterious road, and it turned out that it was not all that mysterious. The road was very much there – but buried under tons of landslide! That reminded me of the headline imagined by P G Wodehouse about a bunch of labourers buried in a landslide – SONS OF TOIL UNDER TONS OF SOIL.

So, the way forward was to go down the slope to the river bank, where the landslide had petered out, cross the moraine there, and get back on to the road. We looked down at the indicated path with distaste. Even bawa's ardour for bad roads and off-roading was running low by this time.

How far was Padum from here? We asked.

Not too far, he said encouragingly – Only 60 kms!

Bloody hell! Damn and blast! Was this Padum on wheels that it kept getting further away as we came closer and closer? The bloody place was playing with us, like a playing dog who doesn't want to be caught and put back on the leash- it waits until you come close and then runs away further, but not out of sight – and grins and wags its tail at you.

We let the truck go on ahead so that we could follow it, and watched with horror as he crossed the landslide swaying like a drunken sailor, and then plunged into a stream to cross it. The water level came up to above the wheel levels, before he pulled himself out of the water like a buffalo after its bath.

How wonderful! Another water crossing in freezing meltwater. Fantastic. We got soaked again.

We crossed the water, with another growled warning to Adi not to get into neutral gear in the middle of the water. There was no drama like last time, only the inevitable getting wet part. We overtook the truck again and raised a hand in thanks, and he tootled in response.

The road went on and on and on, and we were totally fagged out. The dirt track road had scraped our bums into shreds and shattered our backs into bits, and the repeated dunking in cold water had shrunk our balls into ball bearings. The wet shoes and socks were feeling like blocks of ice, especially as it became colder after sunset, and I was wondering about how many toes I would lose to frostbite by the end of the day.

Suddenly, Adi screeched to a halt and seemed to take a swan dive to the floor!

WTF! Did he faint and fall down or what?

But no – He suddenly saw that the road was tarmac, and he was overcome with joy and fell to the road to kiss it in gratitude.

'Oh my darling....I had missed you so much...' he sobbed 'I will never mock you again, or go after dirt tracks to do off roading on....boohoohoo...promise never to leave me again...' his tears wet the tar as he desperately tried to French kiss the road and lick it all over.
'Here- get up.' I hissed 'The locals will think that you have some weird sexual fetish or something.'
'Nooooo....let me love this black beauty for some more time...muah muah muah' he kissed the road again and again before we could convince him to stop humping the road and get back on his bike. He squealed a bit as his bruised bum hit the seat.
'Where to?'
'There's a J&K tourism bungalow in Padum, like the one in Portukchey. We will stay there.'

We found the bungalow all right, but we also found a big lock on the door! The caretaker had apparently decided to take a sudden holiday, and locked the place and fucked off somewhere.
I stared at it dazedly. My legs were freezing, and my brain was slow as molasses, and that was the only thing that prevented me from giving in to the red mist of rage that descended on me.
Else I would have smashed that lock and broken the door and found that absconding caretaker and disembowelled him with my bare

hands and danced on his remains with my riding boots and burnt the place down and sieved the ashes and smeared my forehead the ashes and howled at moon...

'Excuse me' someone plucked at my sleeve, and then recoiled at my expression as I turned towards him.
'WHAT?'
'You want a room?' he asked hesitantly.

'No, I enjoy standing in front of locked doors in the dark, when I am wet and frozen and hungry and tired and pissed off. This is my hobby, my passion. I rode here all the way from Bombay because I like to look at locked doors'
This is what I wanted to say, but luckily I didn't. Some guys are very literal, and don't get sarcasm.

'Yes....yes...I do want a room.' I replied. 'But there is a lock on this door.'
'Yes sir...the caretakers' gone somewhere. But you can stay in our hotel if you want.'
'The MOTHERFU....er...what's that? You have a hotel?'
'Yes sir...see?' he pointed across the street. 'We have room with hot water.'
'HOT WATER! YOU HAVE HOT WATER! Lead me to the room ASAP.'
I told the guys that we are staying here.
'What's the rent?' Del asked.
'Who cares man? If he asks for my bike, I will give him that also for a warm room and a hot bath right now.'

Padum

The hotel turned out to the Monastery guest house – which meant that it was a hotel operated by the monks of the Karsha Gompa of Padum.

We had slept like the dead after our exertions of the day, and when the raven came to the window in the morning and tried to say UTHO REY, I gave it such a nasty look that four of its feathers burnt off due to the fire in my eye. It gave a startled OOK CA CACA CA sound and flapped off and so escaped being summarily caught and strangled and being eaten by bawa.
Bawa was suffering tandoori chicken deprivation - he hadn't eaten tandoori for 2 whole days!

Finally we got up, and massaged our aching bums tenderly (We massaged our own bums and not each other's….let me make that extremely clear) and finally made our way to the attached restaurant for breakfast.

Once we had some breakfast and some tea inside us, we discussed what to do for the day.
Exploring Padum was obviously there on the agenda, but each of us had some specific tasks as well
'I need to buy sunglasses' Adi said, and we all rolled our eyes. He had lost 2 pairs already, and we were not even a week down. This was going to be a record breaking sunglass losing trip.
'I need to buy a comb.' Bawa said, and we all burst out laughing. As if a comb was going to have any effect on that steelwool on his head. He would need a lawn mower and bolt cutters to make any impact on that hair.
'I need to find a cybercafé' I said, and there was dead silence.

'Why do you need a cybercafé?' Adi finally asked.
'I need to postpone today's meeting.' I replied.
'Meeting? What meeting?'
'Today is Monday, right? We have a weekly review meeting on Monday. All my sales guys will be waiting for me on the con-call – I need to write a mail and cancel the weekly meet and tell them to submit numbers and plans on mail.'
'What shit! Why are you working when you are on leave?'
'I am not on leave re....as far as my team is concerned, I am hard at work.'
'Bastard!' Adi was first scandalised, and then envious. 'I wish I could do that.' He mused.
'Well...you know the story of the rabbit and the owl... the rabbit saw that the owl on top of the tree was sleeping all day long, and was doing no work at all.
Inspired by the owl, he decided to do the same. So he closed his eyes and curled up for a nap – and a fox came and caught him and gobbled him up!
Moral of the story – to do nothing and sleep all day long, you must be at the top of the tree!'

We went out after breakfast and strolled around in Padum market. For such an out of the way location, it had quite an impressive market. It even had a cyber cafe – it was really really slow but it worked and I accessed my office mail and did some officegiri replying to mails and sending out mails.
But when I opened my personal account, the computer whined and smoked and burst open!
UTHO REY! UTHO REY! STOP WASTING YOUR TIME IN PADUM MARKET AND GO AND SEE THE PLACE.
GO TO KARSHA MONASTERY. SAY MY NAME TO THE HEAD MONK.

GO TO SHEELA WATERFALL
GO TO BARDAN MONASTERY
GO TO RARU VILLAGE
GO TO......phussssssssssssssssss...tssrrrk.....tssskkkkkk...phoom! the computer went up in flames! A tremor went through the shop and a fierce wind came and broke all the windows! The satellite dish exploded with the strain of accommodating Bharathi's wrath.
We all ran out of the shop and stood outside panting.
I tried to pay the cybercafé guy, but he pushed the money back into my hands and took to his heels, screaming in terror.
I shrugged and walked back,
'What's up?' Adi asked
'Nothing much. The usual. Mail from Bharathi.'
'Oh. Should have guessed.' He said, looking at the trail of black smoke.
We walked to the market and found a guy selling goggles. Adi tried them on and finally decided on one.
'Better buy a dozen or so.' I said.
'What nonsense!' Adi was stung. 'Why should I buy a dozen?'
'Bugger...' Del broke in 'You have already lost 2 and broken 1. You still have a week and a half to go and several high Himalayan passes. You will definitely do a yamdoot on a few more goggles. Better to buy and keep a few.'
'You guys talk like I am a sunglass executioner.'
'Well...lets look at the facts. You started the ride in Chandigad, where you left your sunglasses behind on the plane. Then the next day you lost your second set of goggles before even reaching J&K.'
'I didn't lose them – I ...er....just kept them in ...an unusual place.'
'Which is.....?' Del asked gently.
'On...my....saddlebags...' Adi answered sulkily.
'Exactly! And then you got on your bike and forgot to pick them up and started riding – with the result that they blew away.'

'That could happen to anybody.'

'True. Then you borrowed my goggles, and the very next day, you did what?'

'I...stepped ...on them. And broke a stick.' Adi said unwillingly 'But that was just unlucky. I bent down and they slid off my nose, and as I bent to pick them up, I lost my balance and had to take a step to steady myself and so I stepped on them by mistake....'

'Which is exactly what I am saying. You are not a bad fellow. You have nothing against goggles – you love and cherish them and clasp them to your bottom...er...I mean to your bosom...But you are not lucky. That is your problem. Unfortunate goggles come to you to die.'

'Fuck off man. I am going to buy this one goggle and one alone. And you will see that not only will it last me the whole trip, but much beyond as well.'

Del shrugged, and Adi selected a goggle and paid the shopkeeper. The shopkeeper handed him the change, and Adi got a bit hassled, with his wallet in one hand and new goggles in the other. So he put the goggles on his forehead as he reached for the change. As he bent his head down to count the change, the goggles fell off his forehead and as Adi tried to clutch at them, he overbalanced and there was a CRACCCKKKK sound as he planted his 11 size boot on that fragile piece of glass and metal.

We went back to the guest house to check on the bikes, and see how they had fared after the ride, and were gratified to see that they were in good shape. Delzad had expressly forbidden us to wash the bikes, but to Adi's discontent.

Adi lived to wash his bike. Every waking hour, he would go his bike, whisper sweet nothings in its ear, take out a cloth and start wiping it. If he was not wiping it, he would take out a tin of wax polish and polish it – his favourite activity was polishing the exhaust in a steady pumping motion as if he was trying to jerk the bike off. Then he would colour the tyres black. Then he would wet his finger and stick it in the exhaust , twisting his finger here and there to give the maximum pleasure. When he thought that no one was looking, he would start to hump the bike lovingly, while caressing the tank. It was the textbook definition of machinophilia.

To tell such a person not to wash his bike, was to break his heart. 'Why?!!' he had wailed indignantly. 'Why can't I wash my lovely lovely bike? Why? Why? Why?'

'Bastard – you will dump a bucket of water on it, and suppose it shorts some electricals? Who is going to repair it in the middle of nowhere? Suppose it enters the disc? Suppose while rubbing it you break a wire or a fuse? This is a Royal Enfield – treat it with care. You never know what reason it will invent to break down. No no no no no no.....no washing it until we get back home.'

Adi sulked and pined, poor fellow, but we were hard hearted and did not allow him to wash his bike. We had to be constantly on our guard, and distract him whenever he saw a bucket and a cloth.

There were a few monks standing around the bikes and admiring them, and we started chatting with them. They were all from the monastery of Karsha, and they were on a duty roster at the guest house. The guest house was the property of the monastery, and they ran it for the benefit of the travellers and the pilgrims who came to see the monastery. The monks worked for free, of course, and the profits from the guest house went back to the monastery. It was a win win for all – the travellers got a nice place to stay and the monastery and local economy got a boost.

We made friends with a young monk – Tenzing Panthuk. He was a plump little fellow, 17 years old and still curious about the outside world. As most of the monks start really young, it is unlikely that it was conscious decision on their part to embrace monkhood, or that it was a religious call. The more likely possibility is that the parents placed the child in the monastery.

The reasons for this could be many – it was a free boarding school for the child, the parents may not be economically able to raise the child – here the child would be fed and educated for free, the parents might have thought that having a monk in the family was good thing, it raised their social status, it raised the social status of the child as well – better to be an acolyte in a respected gompa than to be a penniless urchin in a hardscrabble farm.

Whatever it may be, these children are in a strange place when they grow up. Especially today when TV and internet are ubiquitous – especially with the launch of DTH – their curiosity about the outside world and what they are missing out on, must be huge. Eating gruel and chanting the name of Buddha must be getting old pretty soon when you see scantily clad babes gyrating away on TV when you are 17.

He offered to show us around the monastery and we agreed, taking him with us on the bike. It was a large imposing structure, in the classical style. But in my vulgar opinion, once you have seen one monastery, you have seen them all. It has the same temple with the same paintings and thangkas and the same ochre robed monks floating around.

Bharathi gets really incensed when I say such things.

WHAT DO YOU MEAN ALL MONASTERIES ARE THE SAME, EH? YOU VANDAL...YOU GOTH...YOU PHILISTINE!

That reminded me...I was supposed to meet the head monk and mention Bharathi's name to him. But there was no one here.

I turned to Tenzing and asked him where everybody was, the place was deserted.

'I really don't know...' He shrugged and replied 'in the morning some villager came in babbling something about some Bharathi, and the head monk screamed AAAARRRGHHHH and had a fit, and when he recovered he declared a holiday and everyone rushed out of the gate in a cloud of dust.'

Adi and Del turned to look at me and I just shrugged. They also shrugged and said 'Chalo, accha hai. We can see the place in peace.' After we finished seeing the place, Tenzing invited us to his room for a cup of tea and we accepted gladly. I was curious to see how a monk lived.

Quite luxuriously, I must say. Comparatively speaking, of course. He had a little room to himself, with electric lighting. He had an LPG gas and burner. He had a small TV and VCD player. I was impressed that a young monk of little seniority was able to live like this, and suspected that his seniors probably did not know about it. But he was very hospitable and told us about himself. His family was from Zanskar, a day or two from Padum, and he had been in Karsha monastery since he was a child.

We finished our chai and gave him some money as a present. He tried to decline, but we insisted and finally he accepted gratefully. It must have been a rare thing for him to have cash money.

We dropped him back to the guest house, where he went to the restaurant and loftily ordered a plate of mutton momos. The senior monk who was acting as manager raised his eyebrows at this, but served him anyway. Tenzing calmly ate his food, and then went to the surprised monk and dropped a 100 rupee bill on the till, causing his eyebrows to shoot up even more.

'Keep the change' he said loftily, and then took to his heels as the senior monk jumped up and tried to grab him, and everybody in the hotel chuckled.

We went off to explore the area around, and more importantly – to fill fuel! Our tanks were empty after yesterdays ride and we urgently needed to tank up.

'It's just there...' the locals said, pointing down the road. 'just a stones throw away.' We went a fair way down the road, but no sign of a petrol pump. Puzzled, we stopped and asked another local, and he pointed back at the road where we had come. 'Just there...' he said 'five minutes.'

Strange – how did we miss it? We turned back and went back the way we had come – we drove and drove and stopped when we hit the point where we had met that first local. WTF. Where is that pump?

'I can't believe you missed the pump.' Del jeered at Adi. 'Don't you have eyes?'

Adi bristled. 'Why me? You were riding too! Why didn't you see it?'

'Arre, I was just following you.'

'I was following this fatso. He was riding in front. He should have been looking out!' They both turned on me, and I spread my hands in disgust.

'What is this? Blind man's buff? Catching cook? Follow the leader? Sure, I was looking out – but I was admiring the scenery too....but even so, its bloody mysterious. Where is that damn pump?'

We turned around again and drove back on that same stretch of road, and imagine our disgust when we ended up back where we met the second local!

'What the fucckety fuck fuckakk!!!!' Bawa expressed himself at great length with depth of feeling. 'I think they are playing a huge practical joke on us. I think those two guys must be hidden somewhere and laughing their guts out at the sight of these three chootiyas from Bombay driving up and down the road.'

'Unlikely that.' Adi said doubtfully. 'Even those guys at the hotel and the gompa also said the pump was here.'

'Then it's a conspiracy! The whole village is on it! All of them must be hidden behind that ridge and laughing at us!' bawa raved.

We turned around again, and went back – this time keeping a snail's pace, so as not to miss anything.

'Aha!' I shouted

No wonder we had missed it earlier. It was the most unobtrusive pump that I had ever seen. There was no signage, no building, no customers – nothing! There was just a small pump in the ground and a shabby white Maruti 800 parked there.

And it turned out that we were just in time too! Because it turned out that the owner of the pump was in that Maruti, and was about to leave for the day.

We lined up in front of that anonymous pump, and Del opened his tank and waited. The pump operator put the nozzle into the tank and told Del 'Here...hold this nozzle steady.'

Del was surprised. 'If I hold the nozzle, what will you do?'

'I will turn the pump, of course.'

As we watched goggle eyed, he put the meter to zero by simple expedient of pushing the dials with his finger, then he picked a lever from the top of the pump, inserted it into the pump and started to turn it round and round!

Wow! A manual pump! I had heard of such things – in novels about world war 2 – but this was the first time I had seen one. That was so cool!

After we finished filling up we went to check out Sheela waterfall.

It was a very pleasant ride in the country, it was green and hilly and the air was fresh and the sun was shining. We passed a bunch of kids just going home from school, and gave 3 of them a lift to home – Sheela village. It turned out to be quite a distance – I was impressed at the sheer distance these kids walk to get to school every day. The water fall was right inside the village – it was quite nice too.

When we got back, we were still a bit stiff and saddle sore from yesterday, and were not looking forward to repeating the ride tomorrow.

To my surprise, this was the opinion of the other two as well! They started babbling about putting the bikes in a truck back to Kargil. In fact, they had already found a truck driver willing to take us and had closed the deal with him! We were going back by truck.

'Et tu Brutes! Arre mere gabru jawan!' I cried 'Laanat hai tumhare jawaani pe! What a pair of wimps you are!'

Adi bristled. 'What do you mean 'wimps' bugger? You were the one crying about riding!'

'I am allowed to be a wimp.' I replied. 'I am old and grey and fat and lazy. What about you?'

Both of them muttered something and went off, hiding their shame in their headscarves.

That night we ate and drank with abandon – well as much abandon as you can have in a monk-run guest house, and a bawa with AMS and an Adi with PMS.

Padum to Kargil

The next morning we packed our saddlebags, and the two amigos went off to find the truck wala.

'Let's not be late, else that truck fellow might worry about getting late and run off.' Del said as he rushed off.

The poor fellow must have really suffered in the ride with a mix of upset tummy and Altitude sickness. His upper end and lower end were both rumbling – his head had throbbed with AMS and his ass had throbbed with diarrhoea. Not to mention his legs freezing by soaking in the water crossing. Else, I can't imagine anything he would have enjoyed more than riding for 500 km on fucked up dirt roads. Poor fellow. Now he was the driving force in this movement to load bikes in trucks! Amazing. That rajma rice must have been really something.

I was feeling really weird that morning. It took me sometime to realise the reason. There had been no Bharathi call in the morning. No phone call, no crow, no hotelier – no one. AAH. What a relief! Maybe she has got a sore throat or something.

I wondered exactly how does a bike enter a truck? You don't appreciate how high a truck cabin is until you are considering putting a 200 kilo bike into it. It's bloody high up. Even hauling my 100 kilo ass on to it would be a task – hauling a reluctant dead weight of a bike only it sounds like truly a herculean task – requiring either a single demigod Hercules or at least several human myrmidons.

No coolies were likely to be available this early in the morning, and if we tried to do it ourselves, the peace of the morning was likely to be punctured by the 'pop pop' of our intestines bursting through our hernias and nestling companionably along with our testicles and the musical screams of the owners of the said testicles.

Wondering about all these things, we turned up at the rendezvous point, but loading the bikes in the truck turned out to be unexpectedly easy. There was a helipad in Padum, with a ramp specifically built for vehicles to be loaded, I suppose. The truck lined up in front of it, and it was just a matter of riding the bike into the truck. Then they tried their best to tie up the bikes as securely as possible, so that they would not fall over and crash due to the bad roads. Bawa, Adi and the truck guy all produced ropes, and the inside of the truck had hooks and stuff to tie the ropes on, and they proceeded to tie the bikes like a cop tying up a suspect, so that he would not escape. The bikes were festooned with ropes, and looked like flies caught in a spider web. I didn't even enter the truck body – there was so much rope and testosterone sloshing around – they would have tied me up too.

Unfortunately, they sucked at tying knots – so the bikes came loose after a few minutes and spent the journey banging against each other. They would have sustained less damage had we driven down!

We all clambered into the truck driver's cabin, and I looked around with interest. It was the first time that I had been inside a truck. It was a baroque design, with all the comforts that the guy could afford. A music system, a sleeping area, baroque wooden panelling inside the cabin – it looked like a seraglio on wheels. It wouldn't have surprised me if a houri popped out from somewhere and started doing a belly dance.

The driver was a jolly looking Jammu fellow (what do you call people from Jammu? Jammies?) and his cleaner was an amiable Kashmiri lad, 17 years old. Wow, I thought – another 17 year old. First that Lama, now this mama.

We started off on the truck ride and it was an exciting moment! My very first truck ride! After so many days of looking at trucks as 'The enemy' – the guys who wanted to kill you and crush you to bits at the first opportunity – it was a bit weird to be part of it. Must have been how the guys in East Germany must have felt when they merged with West Germany after the wall fell. The truck driver also must looked at bikers as irritating cockroaches who deserved to be crushed into a fine paste, but here we were – in the same cabin, smiling hesitantly at each other.

This truck driver was not just the driver – he was also the owner, and also a businessman and entrepreneur . He was, in fact, a true descendant of the old silk route caravans– he would bring supplies from the plains of Jammu all the way to the mountain fastnesses of Ladakh and Kargil and Padum and where in olden days he would have been paid with gold and saffron and pashmina wool, he was being paid with grubby currency notes. The brightly painted and caparisoned truck was his camel train, and the gangly teenager was his shield carrier and apprentice. We were the brave knights joining a caravan to add to its strength, though maybe he was looking at ways to enslave us and sell us in the great slave markets of Ludhiana. (There used to be a great slave market in Ludhiana in the Mughal days. Now there are only sardars selling machine parts...quite apt actually – machines are the slaves of today)

He would stop at all the shops and honk away and all the shopkeepers and traders would come running down to pay him and place orders for stuff they wanted. He would drop off the goods on the way up, and collect payment on the way down; and as he was the only source of supplies in the region, no one would try to renege on payments.

As soon as the commerce was over, he handed over the reins to his apprentice and went to the back of the cabin for a nap. This kid wasn't even old enough to have a license to drive a scooter and here he was driving a humongous truck over the mountains. He grinned at us and we grinned back.

The absolutely amazing views of the ranges were before us, and it was a different perspective from inside that truck. You weren't freezing in the cold wind, and were at a much higher position from the road. The shock absorbers of the truck were obviously much stronger than a bike, so the truck could go much easier over the bad roads – but this caused us to wince in agony as we imagined what was happening to the bikes in the back. Adi was looking like a guy who's wife is in labour – he was all white and tense and was chewing his nails and kept trying to look behind him.

As we approached the pass, the trucker woke up and took over, as an expert hand would be needed to tackle the high pass. He stopped the truck and went to wash his face in a stream and ordered the kid to make some tea.

Tea? I wondered how he was going to make tea, and I was fascinated to see that they had fixed up a full size gas cylinder in the truck and had attached a long tube which he attached to a small stove and made a pot of piping hot tea. I loved this truck - it had a bed, a music system and even a cooking apparatus. This guy was really organised.

Then he stretched and cracked his fingers and got into the drivers seat to tackle the tough part of the climb. He sweated and struggled with the wheel while we relaxed and enjoyed the views of the Darang Durung glacier.

'Look look' me and Adi would point to each other 'That is where bawa went zooming down!'

'Look look – that rock is where he dropped his bike and ran'

'And that is the place where he crapped his guts out – Look , the whole place has turned black and rotten – even the birds and animals are avoiding the place...see the skeletons of the unfortunate souls who got too near and were killed by the smell!'

'His shit stained hanky must be fluttering somewhere on the hills. Just imagine – if scientists find it in the future, they can clone a new bawa.'

'Fuck you guys' Bawa growled, holding his head. The motion of the truck was making him sick. He can drive over the roughest roads, but when he sits in the passenger seat, it makes him carsick.

The truck bravely struggled through the pass and again I felt that we had taken a lazy but wise decision to take the truck. The road was completely underwater in some places, and it had become muddy and awful. We saw some bikers coming in the opposite direction and they were really struggling.

'This road is not for bikers at all' The trucker cribbed 'You can do it once for an adventure, I suppose...but its a silly idea all the same.'

We left that wild mountain road behind finally and stopped to rest and refuel. I watched with interest as he filled the tank with kerosene instead of diesel. Bad for the engine, but so much cheaper. The government heavily subsidises kerosene as it is a cooking fuel for poor people, and due to this it is very cheap. This tempts people to use kerosene in all kinds off engines, even those designed for petrol and diesel. This screws the engine and causes air pollution, but saves money in the short term. To prevent this adulteration, the government adds a blue colorant to kerosene and has a whole police structure to catch people using kerosene. The total effect of this stupid subsidy is that it perverts the entire fuel market and aids corruption everywhere. It might be a much simpler idea to keep Kerosene at its natural price and let the market adjust to using whatever fuel suits it best. This might give rise to use of solar ovens and bio gas etc - which are cheap and user friendly.

Adi and Bawa went to check on the bikes and then decided to ride on the roof of the truck. I was too fat to climb up, so I pretended that it was below my dignity to climb up on roofs like a monkey and stayed put in the cabin. Riding on the roof was obviously a bad idea, as these two morons discovered after getting slapped in the face by tree branches and almost getting beheaded by overhead wires – not to mention getting dust in the face, getting frozen and almost falling off. Soon they were back in the cabin – shamefaced and blackfaced – with me smirking at them.

The road went ever on and it was dark by the time we approached Kargil. The truck would not be allowed in the town in the night time, and so he would be taking some bypass. He went slowly, looking for a place to unload the bikes but couldn't find anything. Finally he stopped near a pile of soil that someone had dumped, and backed up the truck to it, making it a makeshift ramp.

Makeshift indeed! It was a pile of dirt! I stood there looking at it doubtfully, but bawa gave a whoop of joy and went and untied his bike and came and drove it straight out and down that slope of dust. He was so overjoyed that he grabbed the keys of our bikes and drove them down too. He was about to ride his bike back up inside and down a couple of times, when the trucker got worried and moved off, leaving behind a sad bawa. Me and Adi were shitting at the thought of dismounting bikes from the truck, but bawa loved the whole experience.

What a relief it was to get out of the smelly cramped truck, and on to our bikes. Woo hoo. This was the way to travel. The truck interlude was just a momentary lapse.

We roared into town and went hotel hunting. I remembered Kargil as a sleepy little shitty town, where I got bit by bedbugs – but now the place was rocking. Hotels everywhere! And all overpriced!

We went to some fancy hotel and I gasped when he quoted some three and a half thousand bucks. And he refused to bargain or come down on the price. 'Be reasonable' I told him 'It's late at night, and you are not going to get any more guests coming to you. Rather than letting your room go empty and making zero money, give me the room for a thousand bucks. That's a thousand more than you are making right now.' But no. He put his head down like Balaam's ass and refused to listen to reason.

'Well then, fuck you.' I said and walked out. Adi and Delzad gasped and clutched each other and started crying bitterly. 'OOOOO .... where will we sleep tonight....we are tired....and scared of the dark....and you will make us sleep on the street...OOOOOOO' they wailed.

'Here...relax' I said 'Don't worry about it. I will show you how we great backpackers manage'

And as if on cue, one local sidled up to me and said, 'Saar – you want room? Cheap room?'

Of course we wanted a cheap room, and we went off with him to see the room. It was an OK room, but without an attached bathroom - we would have to use a common loo. Which was fine with me, but Adi was very disturbed by this somehow, and spent the whole night guarding the bathroom and not allowing anyone else to use it. He was like a dog guarding a gate, and would have probably bitten anyone who tried to use it.

We went off for a nice dinner and crashed happily for the night.

The Zanskar adventure was over...now to head to Leh!

Kargil to Leh

It had been Adi and Del's first experience of budget hotel, so they had approached the bed with some distrust – but add a bit of Old Monk to the mix and all problems are solved. Adi forgot about his goal of standing outside the loo all night and preventing anyone else from using it – but he did put his alarm to wake him up at the crack of dawn so that he could use the loo before anyone else so that his butt crack would touch a pristine surface, untouched by human buttocks. It was a win-win as far we were concerned, he got to use an untouched seat, and we got a nice warm seat to sit on.

My phone rang early morning with a loud noise and it started emitting black smoke and made a buzzing sound as if it was going to explode so I knew that this was a call from She-who-must-be-obeyed. Her clarion call echoed through the room, waking up bawa and all the other denizens of the hotel with a jerk.

'UTHO REY! UTHO! GET UP! GET UP! UP AND AT THEM!'

'Yeah yeah...' I grumbled 'We are up. In fact Adi got up even before you called...' and I bit my tongue. Shit. I shouldn't have said that. Now she would be insulted and start calling even earlier.

'GET UP AND START MOVING! YOU ARE IN THE MOUNTAINS. YOU NEED TO CROSS PASSES BEFORE NOON!'

That word 'NOON' was so powerful that Adi's bowels expelled with a jerk, making him feel all light and airy – he had been straining on the pot since dawn – and faster than time could tell, we were on the bike and moving.

It was such a huge difference between the Kargil-Padum road, and the Kargil-Leh road. There was tarmac – such beautiful, newly laid tarmac. It was a pleasure to ride on – you could speed, take steep turns and banks, sheer riding pleasure. The views were awesome – AWESOME – and the roads were great. Also, there was much more traffic. It was quite weird to see so many vehicles and people on the road after the Zanskar experience.

This is truly God's own country – I can't even to begin to describe the beauty of the place. The area around Kargil is green and cultivated, and then the Himalayan desert begins. Gloriously blue sky – a sky we can't even imagine in the polluted plains – amazing!

And the mountains – what to say about the mountains? What can one say? They affect you so deeply. They are painted in all kinds of crazy colours – as if the artist was on an acid trip. Now we know that the colours are because of presence of mineral elements – science blablabla – but it is so fantastic...the painted mountains, the blue sky, the white clouds, the bright green of the cultivated fields , the riotous wildflowers wherever there any presence of water...its unearthly.

And when the roads are so good that you can really ride your motorcycle and watch this beauty whizz by in a beautiful blur, it is really a religious experience. The roar of my Enfield, the feel of the powerful bike vibrating and revelling in the roads, the scream of the wind in my helmet, the feel of the sun in my face, the presence of friends with you who are enjoying the same experience, the beauty of the surroundings – its as close to a perfect experience that you can get.

PHURRRRRR - a derisive noise came in my head and I nearly fell off my bike! WTF – now She was talking straight inside my head.

WHAT NONSENSE – THE REAL THRILL IS IN DOING THIS ROAD ON CYCLE. YOU ARE FAT WIMPS WHO CAN'T POWER THEMSELVES SO YOU ARE GOING ON MOTORCYCLE

'Oi! Get out of my head! You nearly made me fall off.' I complained.

The first village on that route is Mulbek and you know you are getting there when you start seeing some agriculture happening – green fields and yellow mustard flowers. There is a huge Buddhist bas relief carved out of rock of the Buddha (what else?) doing various stuff. It looks exactly like an ancient Hindu god carving from the posture – you know the old style posture of the guy standing slightly teda – and its got 4 arms holding Hindu stuff like a kamandalu water pot, rudraksha beads, some axe or flail kinda thingy, and one arm just pointing down. Its wearing a rudraksha belt and got a snake around it and the hair is matted...basically a statue of Shiva like the ones you will see all across India – only here the face is of the Buddha. Probably the newly converted Buddhists wanted to make a statue of the Buddha but the artisans were trained to make only Shiva carvings. Or possibly they started making a Shiva carving, but then the boss converted to Buddhism or they were conquered by a Buddhist tribe and just changed the face and called it Buddha instead of Shiva.

I wanted to stop and admire it – but these two morons just zoomed past.

Adi – Mr Perpetual Motion himself – could stop himself and was just zooming and bawa was racing him. 'Can't stop! Gotta move!' were his watch words. He just refused to get off his bike, he would drink water from his Camelback while in motion and would even pee in motion – he would just stand up on the pegs unzip and go wizzz all over the road. He would have been really happy as a horseman in the Mongol hordes where they would keep riding for days on end – just jump from horse to horse when they were tired and cut a vein on the horse and drink its blood when they were thirsty or hungry, like a horse vampire!

'Go slow you fucker' I told him 'Enjoy the scenery. You will never see anything like this again.'

'You are going as fast as I am' He replied, stung. ' Even faster.'

'Yes – but I have been here before and seen the place.' I replied.

'Then what are you complaining about?' he retorted and zoomed off.

After Mulbek the next main place would be Lamayuru – a lovely monastery. But before that we would be crossing not one, but TWO high passes – Namik La at 3760 metres and Fatu La at 4147 metres.

Namik La is just 15 Km from Mulbek, and was a major obstacle in the old days – but now with the BRO maintained roads and powerful bikes, its not a problem. But you have to treat passes with respect as SHE-who-must-be-obeyed said – cross them early in the day before the bad weather strikes. Anything can happen on the passes at any time – fog, rain, snow... just check out the message boards in Team BHP for various experiences people have had.

There is a high pinnacle of rock at the pass which has given the pass its name – 'Namika' means 'Pillar in the sky', and there was a sign by the Border Roads Organisation saying 'Namika La –Altitude 12198 feet' and we all took photos in front of it proudly.

On the way down I saw a fallen woman.

Well, a fallen biker....to be precise a fallen bike, with an embarrassed looking biker trying to lift the bike and failing. When I stopped to help, it turned out to be a woman – a 'bikerni' from Pune. Picking up a fallen Enfield is no joke, and has to be done in a certain way – you have to come between the bike and the road and push – not stand at the other side and pull as she was trying. You have to be built like King Kong to pull a bike up.

She was the last person in the group and the rest had gone on ahead, not even knowing that she had fallen. She must have been notorious for riding slow and stopping for photos so no one was going to wonder about her for quite some time, and she might be there still but for me! Or maybe she was a yakking bitch and they were glad to be rid of her for some time…who knows?

I picked her up...picked her bike up, to be precise, and she thanked me and zoomed off. She must have caught up with her friends and given them an earful after that. All of her friends wanted to thank her saviour, but they identified wrongly and they all waved at Adi lovingly and thanked him and confused him utterly. He got so scared that maybe his sexual magnetism was acting up again or his ass was looking so good that all these bikers had got the hots for him, that he throttled up even more and ran away as fast as his bike could carry him.

After Namika la, we descended down to Bodhkarbu – which is a tiny no-horse town, but has an interesting story. The Cannibal dude – whom I spoke about earlier – used to live near Bodhkarbu. He used to entice travellers into his hut with promises of hospitality and then murder and eat them. You can just imagine him making a completely factual invitation to 'come in for a bite'.

There is a nice little picnic spot before the next pass, and we stopped there for a break and for enjoying the scenery. We just getting into the zone and thinking beautiful thoughts, when the whole atmosphere was polluted by a gaggle of gujjus in an Innova. Gujjus – lovely people generally – are a real pest and pollutant if you want peace and quiet. The high pitched cackling totally screwed the mood and we ran away from the place. The best thing about Gujjus is the food they carry with them – you can't go wrong with thepla and farsan – and I hung around them hoping for some handouts. They finally gave me some to make me go away.

Between horny bikers and potential cannibals and noisy gujjus, Adi was in terror until we left Bodhkarbu behind and came to the other high pass – Fatu la. This is at 4147 metres and that is a really respectable height – and is the highest point on the Srinagar – Leh road. BRO has put up a nice yellow sign there proclaiming the fact, and like all high passes in Buddhist lands, the place is covered with prayer flags.

Prayer flags are a pretty interesting idea – they are small cloth flags with 'Om mani padme hum' printed on them in bright gay colours, and the Buddhists believe that when the winds pass through them they blow the blessings about with them wherever they go. I thought it was a really charming thought.

With the power of the 500 cc enfield, we barely noticed the strain of the climb and after the obligatory stop and photo session, we descended down to Lamayuru.

Now, this is the THE landscape you want to be riding in. It is a spectacle like no other.

It is called 'Moonland'.

The ground here is brown – utterly devoid of vegetation – and twisted into weird and surreal shapes – 'Loess' if you want the correct geological term. It looks like ….the surface of the moon..duh

– that's why its called Moonland. Even Mr Perpetual Motion was impressed enough to go a bit slow.

The famous thing in Lamayuru is the Lamayuru gompa, or Buddhist temple. This is one of Ladakh's most famous and supposedly the oldest Buddhist monastery. Its officially known by the cool name of 'Yung dung therpa ling'. Legend wise, there was a lake here, inhabited by snake demons, and some Buddhist dude kicked the demons out and then the lake dried up and left this moonland behind. The gompa was built in the 11th or 12th century, and by the 15th century had become the power in the land, with the monks being traditional consultants to the kings of Ladakh. In fact, it was given autonomy and the power to give sanctuary to the criminals who came to it – the name 'Therpa ling' actually means 'place of freedom'.

Even today it is an important monastery and is inhabited by 150 odd monks, and has a lot of cool stuff – like the cave of Naropa which has the mummy of the ascetic Naropa, hand painted 108 volumes of the Buddha's teachings, lots and lots of statues and paintings of Avalokiteshwara, Tara, Vairochana and a lot of confusing Buddhist imagery which is gory and weird. Lots of weird demons and naked wretched people being tortured or eaten and stuff.

When I came here first, it was quite a sleepy place, but now they are very touristy – with a fancy restaurant and places to stay and whatnot. Its all run by the monastery, so its good income for them – but the sleepy tranquil atmosphere is gone now. We had lunch there and Bawa was shocked to meet a school friend of his there.

'I never see the fucker in Thane' he said 'But I meet him in Lamayuru. So weird.'

After a rather unsatisfying lunch, we left the monastery and started the last leg of the journey to Leh.

Leh is in a valley, and so the road wound steadily downwards – in fact it goes spectacularly downwards in a series of 18 hairpin bends which are a real thrill to ride on – you lean into the turn and try to go into as deep an angle as possible – the aim is to scrape the footpegs and make sparks fly! That KHRRR sound is what makes the day! We really had a ball going down those loops.

These loops are named after a cow. The cow apparently slipped and fell at the top of the hill and fell directly down to the last loop. Cow is 'hangroo' in Ladakhi and that is how the cow got immortalised and the locals presumably got a steak dinner and some new shoes.

The Enfield Bullet is called a 'Bull' and so I suppose there is some poetic justice in Bulls hurtling down the Cow loops.

After Hangroo loops we crossed Khaltsi where some river rafting expeditions start and then comes Nimmu – Which is where you can see the awesome sangam of Indus and Zanskar rivers. We stopped there and drank it in. Drank the sights, not the rivers. That would be silly. The bright blue Zanskar merges into the somewhat muddy Indus, in a completely bare land.

Rivers. Moonland. Blue sky. Clouds. Silence. Bikers. Thump.

Godliness.

With some reluctance, we moved on from Nimmu and just a short way onwards was the Patthar Sahib Gurudwara.

Its called Patthar sahib because there is a huge rock there, with the imprint of a sitting human figure in it. The legend is that Guru Nanak was supposed to have been sitting there in meditation, when a demon decided to have some fun and crush the sitting human by rolling a huge boulder on to him. The huge boulder came thundering down, but when it touched Guru Nanak it turned as soft as wax and stopped there, presumably leaving the demon as sick as mud and gnashing his teeth in frustration. The imprint of his body was left on the rock and we can see it to this day.

This used to be a small and obscure place till the Indo Pak and Indo China border issues started, and a lot of army battalions started being posted there. The army is full of serds, and having nothing better to do out there, they adopted the gurudwara and spent a lot of money maintaining it – the various battalions competed with each other to do stuff for it, and it has become an important place.

Like all gurudwaras, it is clean and well maintained, and they serve tea and boondi as langar prasad there. Adi felt very nice there because of the plethora of bearded gurus and he stood there and stroked his beard proudly and sneered at the beardless fools that he was travelling with.

The next attraction is the great con of the 'Magnetic hill'. That point has become very famous, and the BRO has even put up a big yellow board saying 'Magnetic hill'. The local people and guides give you some bullshit about how vehicles roll upwards against gravity and water flows upwards instead of downwards. All crap – don't believe a word of it. There was one guy in a car trying to show tourists that water was flowing upwards, and he got pissed when we laughed at him and showed him that it was flowing downwards.

'Its going up, I tell you' he protested.

'Balls.' I replied and proved it to him by putting on a 'level' app on my phone and showing him the angle of the ground. He turned purple and zoomed off before his clients could beat him up and demand a refund.

Magnetic hill, my ass.

The traffic on the road increased as we neared Leh, but it was a long way off still. There are number of signboards saying proudly 'Welcome to Leh' but they are all a false dawn. We stopped happily at the first one and took photos, and got steadily cheesed off as we passed a number of other 'Welcome to Leh' signs. Adi was remembering the Padum road, where it kept getting further and further the more we rode.

But finally we passed the airport and came to the town and I actually remembered the route from there!

It's incredible that I remembered the route, because I am a complete moron when it comes to remembering roads. I regularly get lost on the way home, and passerby must got used to seeing a fat guy staring confusedly around him. Its like a weird form of dementia or something.

But this road I remembered, but to the surprise of the Amigos, and they followed me somewhat bemusedly as I roared into town.

We went into the bazaar, and even before we could start looking for a hotel, we were collared by a local.

'You want room?'

'Yes.'

'Come with me. I give good room for low price.'

'OK. Lead on MacDuff' I said

Adi was scandalised! This was no way to take a room! The way to take a room was to see a hundred places, ask searching question, agonise over the decision, and go into a loop of uncertainty. How can we just take a room like this?

He plucked at my sleeve. 'How can we just go with him? Is it safe? What if he wants to ravish us and rape us and loot us and eat us like the cannibal in Bodhkarbu? What will I say to my parents if I get killed and eaten, eh? Have you thought of that? Have you? Have you?'

But we just ignored him and carried on and he followed us sulkily.

The guest house was called 'Dorje guest house' and that guy was the eponymous Dorje. The room was fine – a nice B&B where the family lived on the ground floor and they had built a couple of floors for guests. We fixed up the terms and got settled in.

After we had got freshened up, we went to the bazaar for dinner and got really shocked. After the emptiness of the places we stayed in on the Srinagar Padum Leh route, it was a shock to be in such a crowded place. It was like being in fucking Goa. We were so tired and there wasn't even a beer available. We finally found a place in some shitty pizza place –which had a 'stone-fired oven', but had run out of non-veg toppings. Luckily I was carrying a bit of rum, so I was happy.

But these were all minor things. The main thing was that we had arrived. We had completed the Srinagar – Leh ride!

We were Leh bikers now!

I would have thought that we would just chill and take it easy in Leh, but was woken early morning by Dorje.

At least I thought it was Dorje – it looked like Dorje...but that zombie like walk, those jerky hand motions, those terrified eyes...

He opened his mouth and closed it again. HNGH HNNN. He closed his eyes tightly, swallowed once and tried again.

UTHO REY!

I should have known. Poor Dorje.

UTHO RE...UTHO...GET UP.

'But why?' I whined 'Today is a rest day.'

WHAT DO YOU NEED REST FOR? YOU HAVE BEEN SITTING ON YOUR BUTT. ITS A REST FOR YOUR BIKES, NOT FOR YOU.

'Why not for us?'

BECAUSE YOU HAVE TO GO AND GET YOUR PERMITS YOU MORONS! GO TO THE DISTRICT COLLECTORS OFFICE AND GET YOUR PERMIT. AND GET THE BIKES SERVICED. AND DON'T DRINK TOO MUCH. AND DONT....

'Naheeeeen' a wail came from below, and I turned and saw Dorje's wife, mother, mother in law, sister in law, neighbour, driver, washerman all looking at him and pointing. His wife was sobbing, and his mother was throwing holy water around and mumbling 'Om mani padme hum' incessantly. Wailing and weeping and breast beating was imminent.

OH BUGGER. I WILL SEE YOU LATER. GET THOSE PERMITS DONE.

And Dorje fell down like a puppet with his strings cut and started foaming at the mouth.

Bawa came out scratching his balls and looked at Dorje curiously.

'Bharathi?'

'Yep.'

'Thought so.' He went back inside and fell on top of Adi. 'AAh'

'Hey, stop that. Lets get going before she sends any more after us. See – that crow is acting all weird.'

Leh used to be a sleepy little town earlier, but now with increased tourism is becoming a hell hole like all Indian hill stations. It was the capital of the region and there are a couple of palaces and a polo ground and Shanti Stupa and all kinds of crap places to see. I had seen all of them earlier, and wasn't particularly keen on seeing them again.

The Amigos were interesting only in their bikes anyway, and without me to push them, they had no interest in seeing the sights.

My bike was fine – it was brand new anyway – and needed no particular servicing. But any bike belonging to these two begins breaking down immediately.

Adi's bike in particular was like the ship of Theseus – every part in it had been changed, and was in effect a new bike. Even the frame had been changed. But he ensured that something or the other was breaking down on it – he didn't feel comfortable unless something was creaking or clicking or groaning on his bike.

'Yaar bawa...'

'Hmm?' Bawa was playing with his hair. They looked like they had grown a couple of inches already. Because they were so tightly curled, we had no idea how long they actually were. He would be having an afro like a 70's black movie extra by the end of the trip.

'I think my front wheel bearing is acting up. It might break anytime.'

'Really? Thats fantastic!' he jumped up happily. He was a born tinkerer, and had carted a lot of tools a long way and was keen to use them. He had all the ghoulish pleasure of an enthusiastic doctor when someone had a really bad compound fracture.

'But let us go and get the bike serviced first.' Leh was after all the only place on the whole road with a Bullet mechanic.

We went off to the mechanic and found the place swamped with bikers! Every bulleter in the country seemed to have come to Leh, and all of them were trying to get their done first. It was a melee in there, like a crowd in a Kumbh mela. Hordes and hordes of villagers who scoff at pussy ideas like lining up and discipline and stuff, and know that the way to get the blessings is to barge in and collect before the good stuff is gone, and thats why the good lord gave them stout limbs and sharp elbows for – to push and shove and elbow your way into the temple.

The parallel was quite exact – the bikers were pushing and shoving to their deity – the mechanic – and his blessings on their bikes.

Much like I had done in the Kumbh mela, I decided that I don't need this shit and exited and sat outside and watched the crowd interestedly.

Adi and Del were more of the elbow and stout limbs persuasion and rolled up their metaphysical sleeves and waded in, and emerged a few hours later – bruised and bloodied, but happy – having done whatever tweaks they wanted.

After that we went to another melee – the government office to get the 'Inner line permit' to enable us to visit places near the border - Pangong lake, Tso Moriri lake, etc. I thought it will be a serious affair where steely eyed security men would examine us and our bona fides and see whether we were any threat to the border security. Maybe they would take our fingerprints and retina scans and DNA strands and see if we matched any terrorist or secret agent links.

Nothing could be further from the truth. It turned out to be a shitty little government office with a couple of bored staff sitting there. They didn't even have the forms for the ILP, and instead directed us to the nearby photocopy shop where the guy sitting there was doing roaring business peddling photocopies of the form at ten bucks a pop.

When we wrote where we were planning to go, and even those we weren't planning to go (just in case) and then entered the melee to get these forms stamped and signed and paid some huge government fees, and that was it.

What a useless procedure, and what a useless document.

Typical government idiocy – national security, my ass! Hey Collector of Leh - if you are reading this …you are an asshole.

But at least now we were all done bureaucracy-wise and were all set to explore the rest of Ladakh. Till now my two Ladakh trips had been all about just reaching Leh – and had flown out immediately. Now finally I would be exploring the other parts of Ladakh.

We hung around Leh town after that, just taking in the vibe. It was already a sad shadow of the charming place I had seen 9 years ago, and would no doubt get worse and worse. Increasing domestic tourism is always the death knell – because we Indians are assholes. We have no manners, no civic sense and no sense. Bad manners, bad habits and bad attitude. Part of the problem is the increasing importance of the Amarnath yatra – all the religious assholes who come to Amarnath and pollute the place there think that since they have come so far, they might as well go a little further and see Leh as well, and fuck that place up as well. The other problem is the romance that all the ad agencies have with Ladakh – a lot of ads are shot here, and the place becomes famous and all Indians decide to come and see the place. The movie '3 Idiots' also made the place famous – and inspired a lot of idiots to come here. They come and throw garbage, raise prices, shout and scream and generally screw the place up. Being so close to Delhi is also a liability as every idiot Delhiwala also decides to drive up here to show what a manly man he is, and brings his entire family along to see that.

There were a bunch of Tibetans selling various knickknacks and Adi immediately made a bee-line for the stall selling earrings and bracelets and stuff, and started holding up earrings to his ear and looking at himself in a mirror. He is basically a woman with a beard.

The Tibetan lady conned nicely into buying some trinkets, by batting her eyelashes at him and giving him some sob story about how their season is only 4 months in the year and they survive on what they can sell in those four months.

'You paid HOW MUCH for this?'

'Hey…its made of yak bone and the thread is parachute cord.' He protested.

'You paid HOW MUCH?'

'Er...Yak bone guys! Think Yaks! And thread from actual parachutes.'

'HOW MUCH?'

'Oh fuck you.'

There seemed to be no place to get a drink in Leh, much to my mystification. Finally we gave up, and went to a place to have dinner. Bawa was lusting for tandoori chicken, after so many days on the road. The shock of the Sonamarg tandoori chicken rip-off was wearing off, and we could say the word without wincing.

The blessed bird arrived, and we looked at it with much satisfaction. Ah...that looked good.

'If only there was some beer to have with this chicken, then it would be awesome.' I mused, and was very surprised when the waiter responded 'We do have beer sir – should I bring it?'

'Yes – of course' we replied in chorus. 'Bring it with all possible speed.'

The waiter went off, and came back with a teapot!

We looked at it in confusion.

'Who ordered tea?'

'This is the beer sir' he replied, and poured beer from the teapot! It was as amazing as Jesus changing water into wine! If that waiter had started a religion, I would have converted straight away.

'What is this? Why is beer flowing from a teapot?'

'Actually, we don't have a license to sell beer, and so if the cops see beer bottles on the table we will get into trouble. So we serve the beer in tea pots'

'Oho...I see...then pour away my man – this tea is good for our health'

Replete after a satisfying meal, we made our way back to Dorje guest house, where they all ran away at the sight of us.

'AAAAGh....RUN ....RUN...Bharathi is coming!' They screamed and ran for the hills.

Delzad shrugged and said 'We will have to write a note and tell them that we will be back after our trip to Khardungla pass and Nubra valley'

Khardungla and Nubra valley

UTHO REY ...UTHO REY...UTHO...GET UP...

The familiar words came to me as I shot awake in the morning, but they sounded a little different this time. No zombie hotelier, no crow...who was making the noise? I looked around and saw to my surprise that Adi was trying to slap Bawa awake.

UTHO REY

'Two minutes...five minutes...ten minutes..' Bawa would mumble and burrow back into the sheets, like a bear getting back into hibernation.

UTHO REY.

'Two minutes...five minutes.. please please please'

'What's going on?' I asked, confused.

I JUST THOUGHT THAT I WOULD HELP YOU OUT – WAKING THESE TWO IS QUITE A TASK.

'Oh...don't worry about it...not today. Leave that poor fellow alone. I know just how to get that sleepy bawa out of bed.'

I went over and shouted 'BAWA! We are off to Khardung-la today!'

And BOOM – like a flash, bawa was up! There was crack like lightning, and he was fully dressed and ready, his hair coiling and uncoiling with excitement!

'Let's go!'

IMPRESSIVE.

And Adi fell to the ground and started shaking a bit. Bawa kicked him in the ass and said 'Get up fucker! We are off to the highest motorable road in the world!'

And so we were. The great Khardung-la pass was calling from 5578 meters.

Doing this pass is what all bikers live for. Once you have done Khardungla, you are a man! An alpha male among riders. Doing Khardungla pass is the high point of the entire Ladakh ride.

We set out from Leh early in the morning and reached Phyang, which is the turn off for Nubra valley and K-top (That's what we stud bikers call it - K top) and stopped there at a nondescript dhaba for breakfast, with photos of a plump and buxom Sonakshi Sinha on the wall.

And what a breakfast it was!

He was serving only parathas and dal, and they were among the best parathas I have ever had. As desi and well rounded and ghee filled and appealing as Sonakshi herself!

We ate and ate and gorged ourselves, and only after we stopped and burped that we felt that maybe hogging on heavy parathas isn't the best idea before a high on the highest pass in the world.

But never mind – this breakfast would be worth any queasiness.

Phyang is just 13 kilometers from Khardungla top – but Phyang is at 3600 meters while K Top is at 5578 meters! So in 13 km, you are ascending more than 2000 meters, which is a hell of a climb.

Undeterred, we set off with a roar and attacked that road. We were young and free and mounted on 500 cc Bullets and K Top did not scare us.

Roaring up that road was one of the best experiences of my life.

It is always fun to go up a twisty road on a motorbike, because you can pick up a bit of speed and use the centripetal force to lean the bike at a steep angle for the thrill – and you don't need to use the brakes to slow down – just cut the throttle and the bike slows instantly because it is fighting against gravity. Thus you can have a really thrilling ride, with a greater measure of safety. Of course, conversely, it is bloody scary to come down a steep twisty road.

The other trick with high passes is to do it as early as possible, as the weather always worsens as the day builds up. It becomes cloudy, or foggy and it may even rain. The snows on the high peaks starts melting and all that water comes on to the roads, making it a disgusting muddy slush.

You ideally wouldn't want to experience any of that stuff, so you do it as early as possible. The weather was great – bright and sunny; the mighty Himalayan views, the thump of our bullets, the wind in our face – and the anticipation of doing something great – the highest pass in the world. I was so happy.

The road was in excellent condition, till about 5 km off the summit – this is common to most passes in India – the summit and road near the summit is always in bad shape – and we zoomed up. The bad roads didn't affect us, as we had done Zanskar earlier and soon enough we were on the top.

We had done it! We were on top of Khardungla Pass!

Yahoo! WOOHOO! WE HAD DONE IT! WE WERE ON K-TOP!!

And it was fucking disgusting!

It was like being on bloody Rohtang pass!

It was a bloody chowpatty up there. Throngs of tourists – uncles and aunties and Billus and Bablies – people selling Maggi noodles, shops selling T shirts – it was a bloody picnic spot. I was dumbfounded at the mess. I knew a lot of tourists hire taxis to come and see K top, but I had no idea that it would be this bad. Uncles, Aunties, babies, babas all milling around – the bongs were all wrapped up in monkey caps and shawls and shouting 'Kiii?' to each other, and the punjus were swaggering around in shorts and t shirts and man boobs pretending that this was all normal. All that was missing were the camels and horses which would find in other hill stations.

We were so proud of biking it up here, but the army guys had put up several sign boards of people who had walked up here, cycled up here, ran up here, and even roller skated up here. How the fuck does one roller skate up a slope – especially this much up, over rocks and mud and slush to the highest road in the world? I felt like a total wimp.

'What shit!' I said in shock 'Let's get the fuck out of here.'

'Wait re' both said in unison and jumped off their bikes and started posing in front of the board that said 'You are on Khardung la top – the highest motorable road in the world.' There was already a large group of morons taking selfies in front of the board, but these two just pushed everyone out of the way and started taking their own photos. Limitless amount of photos – with helmet, without helmet, with jacket zipper undone just a bit and then a procession of photos with the zipper coming down an inch in every shot until the jacket was hanging free – looking east, then west, then south, then north, then up, then down – looking in every cardinal point and in a variety of expressions. Adi especially was a photo whore – 'Arre – take my photo na....take it like this na...now like this...now I will hold my helmet in my right hand – now in my left...'

'Fucker...are you a biker or an underwear model?' I growled at him

'Just because you are as ugly as a stump and can't stand looking at your photos is no reason to prevent other people from having their photos taken' Adi shot back shrewdly, silencing me for a minute, and went back to posing.

He probably would have stood there forever, until he was murdered by the hordes of other tourists impatiently waiting their turn for a photo in front of that stupid sign, but for a lucky chance. He tilted his head to jut out his beard and yet give a coy expression, and his sunglasses fell off and he stepped on them with a loud 'CRAACK'

'Number 17' me and Delzad called out together and bowed our head in salute.

'Oh shut up' Adi growled and walked off in a huff to buy another pair of sunglasses. And a Maggi. And a T shirt. And some key chains. And whatever tourist knick knacks he could find.

Finally they deigned to get off the K-top and go down – and about time too. It was after all some serious altitude, and nothing to be taken lightly. All around us were signs warning us about altitude sickness and the fact that it can be fatal – you can develop an oedema (a fancy word for a swelling – doctors love their jargon) in your brain or lungs – and then its good bye. You should not spend too much time at this altitude without acclimatisation, and immediately go to a lower height if you feel sick.

Luckily I have never been troubled by altitude sickness so far, but both of these guys had had a bad time earlier. Already I could see people clutching their heads, and there was one biker who was leaning over his bike and puking away. He needed to get down and see a doctor – luckily he was with a group and they were clustered all around him. I wondered how they were going to get him and his bike down.

The road 10 km on both sides were truly fucked – the tarmac had been stripped off by the ice and ice removal machines, and were all muddy and slushy with the snow meltwater, and were bounded by ice walls on both sides. We were now crossing the Khardung-la top and descending into Nubra valley!

And just as we were descending, I saw a familiar face! It was Indivar Reddy, my friend from Bangalore – one of the guys who inspired me start riding. And he was looking all fucked up with altitude sickness! He didn't even recognise me, and went zooming down the mountain, and off we went in hot pursuit!

Khardungla pass is the gateway to the Shyok and Nubra valleys, and was a part of the old silk road from Leh to Kashgar in central Asia (Now China) which was a big market for Silks and whatever other shit they traded in.

When you descend from Khardungla, you pass North Pullu village – where the non Indian people have to check in with their inner line permits and the Indians go and hog in the various roadside restaurants – and it was in one of these that I found Indi and the gang of ruffians along with him.

'YO INDI.....ASSHOLE, MOTHERFUCKER, COCKSUCKER!!!' I screamed at him, shocking not only him but all the denizens of that hitherto respectable establishment. His friends were so startled that they nearly choked on their aalu parathas and were brought to life by administering the Heimlich manoeuvre or slapping hard on the back.

'KETANNNN – ASSHOLE MOTHERFU....Errrr' Indi stopped in mid greeting as he noticed the blistering looks he was getting from the other guests. 'WHERE DID YOU SPRING FROM YOU BASTARD?'

A couple of the men looked as if they were going to get up and remonstrate with us for the bad language when Adi and Delzad also rode up like the 2 horsemen of the apocalypse and the sight of them frightened them into silence. When Del took his helmet off and showed off his medusa like hair, it turned everyone into stone.

We introduced our companions to each other, and sat down for a meal. The Bangalore boys were the 'Motoholics'. Indi was one of the guys who inspired me to take up riding. He used to be a Royal Enfield man, but now had graduated to better things and was riding a big-ass BMW. But even that was dwarfed by an even bigger ass 1000cc BMW which was being ridden by a big beefy guy who turned out to be a rich planter with farms and estates near Bangalore. Along with them was a bald beefy guy who was trying to balance the lack of hair on his head by growing a ferocious moustache. He looked sad and grumpy, like a bison with a secret sorrow.

'Whats with him?' I whispered to Indi.

'Oh never mind him, he's just had a bereavement so he is a bit upset.'

'Oh my god! Who died?'

'His bike.'

It turned out that he was a tinkerer and bike restorer and had restored a classic pre-war Norton 750 cc bike and against all sensible advice, had decided to ride it to Ladakh. It was like giving an 80 year old grandmother a dose of vitamins and taking her out. You can take her for a gentle stroll around the park with no problem, but if you take her for an orgy and gang-bang her roughly for hours without lubrication and use whips and chains and cigarette butts on her, she is going to conk out midst fuck. And that was what happened – he happily rode it around Bangalore to great applause, but when he took her to Ladakh and started riding her vigorously, she responded with 'Are you fucking kidding me?' and died right in the middle of Zoji La, leaving the poor guy stranded. They had to send the bike off in a truck to Bangalore and rent a bike for him to complete the ride.

So the Norton man was now on a rented Royal enfield and generally pissed with life.

There were a couple of guys more too, but they were like Harold and Kumar ride to Ladakh kind of stuff. They were on a couple of ancient RD350s and seemed to be powered by good karma and marijuana. they didn't have any money, any equipment, any repair stuff and their normal response to any situation was 'Fuck it machaa – lets have a smoke man'.

As usual when two groups meet, both groups compete to tell embarrassing stories about the common acquaintance.

'This fucker!' the bald restorer whispered, pointing at Indi '...This bald bastard...'

'You are bald too machaaa....' the stoner pointed out

'This bald and fat bastard' the restorer amended his statement 'just say the word 'salt' to him. Go on...I dare you ....say the word 'salt'.'

It seemed to be quite an innocuous word to say...I had called him many more words in the past, so I turned to Indi and said 'salt', and to my surprise he turned scarlet and the whole group started laughing like hyenas.

'WHAT THE FUCK MAAAAN??? WHY WOULD YOU SAY THAT WORD MACHAAA???'

'Eh?' I was taken aback by the reaction, and they explained it to me.

'This bastard read somewhere that you should have more salt when you go to high altitudes, and all the way from Jammu he has been after us to eat more salt. Salt salt salt – he even tried to make us put salt in our tea and told us that that is the way that Tibetans drink their tea. Even the rum he was having with a salt rim.

'That's the way to protect yourself from high altitude sickness' he tells us smugly. 'you should be having more salt da.'

But when we got to Leh, he was the first one to start getting dizzy with AMS, so we went to a doctor. She checked him out and said that everything else was fine, but his blood pressure was a bit high - Had he been having too much salt?

Chutiya sala – we all agreed that he is a fool and I immediately suggested we should ride on before Delzad and Adi counter with stories about me.

We finished our lunch and left and decided to ride together for a bit and hit the road to explore the Nubra valley.

This was one of the most beautiful places I had ever seen in my life – the vistas are truly grand, because we are in the great Himalayan range. The sky is so beautiful, and the views are….ah, I sound like a National Geographic reporter. But that is the reason we travel, and go biking in the Himalayas – to get close to the gods.

The Nubra river and the Shyok river flow in this area, and there is plenty of water for grasslands and irrigation and so there is a bit of green rather than the Ladakhi brown, and also the shiny white sands of the deserts.

The Nubra valley forks into a Y , and one end goes to Hunder, and the other end goes to Panamik. There are apparently some hot springs in Panamik, which is fascinating. All hot springs in the Himalayas are fascinating – just think that some underground water is heated by contact with the earths core a zillion miles down and then it fizzes up all the way up to the top of the frozen frikking Himalayas, and be a warm hot tub. It's fantastic.

In the days of the silk road, Panamik was an important stopping point for the caravans before tackling the formidable Karakoram mountains. I can just imagine the caravaners soaking contentedly in the hot springs, relaxing their stiff muscles and then probably getting a nice massage. And a happy ending wank job too, I wouldn't wonder.

Hmmm...sounds so good.

The other fork leads to Hunder, which is famous for having a real Himalayan desert – the term Himalayan desert generally refers to any inhospitable desert landscape where plants can't grow – but this is a real desert with sand and sand dunes and weird Bactrian camels with two humps.

We encountered the Himalayan deserts for the first time – wide sandy deserts with brilliant white sands. It is quite disconcerting to see bloody sand dunes in the middle of the mountains and a pang of sympathy went through me for the merchants who used to travel the silk routes.

Just imagine the buggers' plight, they have come from China and suffered eating grasshoppers and Chinese food, and crossing giant mountains and glaciers and raging rivers and the bad lands of Tibet, and have just heaved a sigh at seeing green valleys and flatter mountains, and are just thinking that the worst is behind them and what do they see? Fucking deserts! Sand dunes and stuff and waiting for them would be double humped camels and crooked camel drivers.

Poor guys.

But the deserts are so beautiful. I just stopped when I saw them, and switched off the bike and just sat there watching the scene. One by one, everyone stopped and we all just sat there watching the scene. It was amazing.

All except Delzad that is. He fell asleep as usual, until we kicked him to wake him up. 'Power nap' he explained, and we nodded.

The original plan was to go all the way to the end of the road – Turtuk – and stay there for the night, but we had wasted a lot of time in the day, what with the meeting up and chatting and looking at sights, and were behind schedule. Also, while you can always find accommodation for 3 people, it may not be that easy to get accommodation for 12 people in a small village. And these guys were not bhikari backpackers like me, but were wanting to stay in a posh place.

And of course, now we had to keep a watch on the fuel situation as well. While me and Del wouldn't have a problem with our 20 litre tanks, Adi surely would – as Enfield in their infinite wisdom, have saddled the Classic with a tiny 12 liter tank, and no fuel guage – so you will know that you are low on fuel only when the bike suddenly dies in the middle of the highway and strands you in the middle of nowhere. On any highway anywhere in India, you will find sad Classic owners standing in front of an empty bike, which is far too heavy to push, and too expensive to leave unattended on the highway.

The only pump in Nubra vallery is in Hunder, so we decided to stay somewhere close to that. I thought that it might be tough to find a place, but increasing tourism interest in the place has sparked off a resort revolution, and we found a nice tented resort to stay in. That resort had a seriously weird location – it was WAY off the beaten track,

There is a place near Hunder where you can see the double humped Bactrian camel, and we wanted to see that, and some guys with expensive DSLRs wanted to take photos of them. I had dreams of a deserted...er...desert...with a herd of camels silently coming up in the evening...romantic Himalayan solitude...silence and the songs of the winds etc. But imagine my disgust when I saw another bloody mela out there. This was actually a fair organised by the local people and villagers from all around had come, and were playing bollywood songs on loudspeakers and local politicians and community leaders were giving speeches and declaring prizes for some local song and dance competitions.

What a disillusionment.

There were a lot of camels though - the place is a tourist attraction, and the local camel herders bring their camels here so that tourists can see them, and for a small fee - have their photos taken with them, or on them. It smacked of being a tourist trap and I refused to go anywhere near them . As far as I am concerned, camels are best seen from afar - their beauty as such is elusive, their gaze is most disrespectful, the neck is too long, the legs too powerful and their teeth are far too big. It can - if so inclined - kick you, bite you, butt you with its head using its long neck, or at least sneer at you with complete contempt. And not to mention that it smells bad.

Apart from having one more hump, I didn't quite see the appeal in them. And anyway, many of them had strangely saggy humps - like the sagging tits of old women. They went flipping and flopping on both sides as the camels moved, and looked most unpleasant.

To be fair, the camels didn't think much of us either, and they sneered at us like only a camel can. Nobody can sneer like a camel. You could imagine them laughing at us for being - variously - old, fat, bald, ugly, unfashionably dressed, stupid, cowardly, etc etc. Not all in one person, but as a collection of qualities.

Nobody could stand the double impact of that mela atmosphere and the camels sneers for long, and even the most dedicated SLR snappers wound up and we went back to the resort.

Now the question was to organise some booze, as you can't expect male interaction without the social lubrication of booze. The lowering of inhibitions is essential to generate the comfort level required for males to interact. Indi was despatched to the nearest town to find booze and he came back bearing it proudly like a flag won in battle.

We swapped riding stories till the rum ran out and then we went to bed. I kept waiting for someone to offer me some weed but no one did, much to my disappointment.

It had been an amazing day! We had done the highest motor able road in the world. Just the three of us and without any help or back up.

Nubra Valley to Leh

The next day we all woke up with mild hangovers due to the rum and the exertions of the ride, not to mention sharing a tent with the smelly Amigos. But just coming out the tent and seeing the place we were in made our hearts sing with joy. We were right on the river bank - so the sound of the river, the incredibly fresh air and the glorious blue sky of Ladakh - all came together to make the day into a fantastic one.

We had earlier planned to go to the end of the road and see Hunder and Panamik and Turtuk and take a dip in the hot springs, and also say 'Hi' to the Air Force base at Thoise, where a cousin of mine had been based for some time. That posting was really extreme - in the short summer time, it was a beautiful place, but in the winter the whole place becomes one gigantic ice box. Khardungla pass gets snowed over and the Nubra Valley is cut off from the mainland. There is an airfield at Thoise, and all supplies are brought in by air. Sometimes the snow is so bad that planes and choppers cannot land there, and the supplies have to be dropped by parachute, and the denizens of Thoise have to go hunting for the parachutes in the snowstorm.

If my cousin had still been based there, I would most certainly have gone and dropped in out there. But they had been posted out just a few months before. And so, I am ashamed to admit, we wimped out of exploring the rest of Nubra valley, and decided to go back to Leh.

A crow came and cocked his head at us, as we discussed how to jettison the plan with dignity.

'We will have to cross Khardungla again and go all the way back to Leh' I said gravely, and everyone else nodded gravely, and Adi stroked his beard gravely. 'One should cross mountain passes early in the day, else the weather can turn bad' I continued gravely.

HAH!

'And there is no difference between this place and Hunder and Turtuk.' Delzad piped up. 'It's the same road, same river, same view, same everything. Nothing new to see.' We all nodded. Yes, theres that, of course. Of course. Nothing new. No sirree.

BLOODY WIMPS! CAW CAW.

'And I believe the baths are quite dirty and nothing much to see there.' Indi said, looking guiltily at the crow. 'We met those bikers who had been there and they said that it was just some ramshackle sheds.'

RAMSHACKLE BIKERS MORE LIKE. CAW CAW. CAWORDS !

'Not even a happy ending' Rajesh said mournfully.

We all looked at him, and he realised that he had said it out loud. Then we all looked at his tent partner, who raised his hands defensively and shook his head vehemently. We shrugged and let it go.

'And its my birthday tomorrow' Adi said 'I am expecting all my girlfriends to call me. How can I receive my calls here? THERE IS NO MOBILE SIGNAL! DO YOU REALISE THAT I HAVE BEEN FOR A FULL DAY WITHOUT A MOBILE SIGNAL? I WANT TO GET TO MOBILE SIGNAL! OR AT LEAST WIFI! I WANT WIFI! I WANT TO POST ON SOCIAL MEDIA! I WANT TO WHATSAPP! I WANT TO INSTAGR....BOOHOOHOOHOOHOO...' he broke off as bawa poured a bottle of water on his head. It was the only way to cool him down when he went on a violent withdrawal from mobile internet. He was a complete junkie and going cold turkey like this affected his mental balance sorely.

He spluttered like a fish as the ice cold water of the Nubra wet his beard, and then came to his senses. 'Its my bud-day... I wanna bud-day' he grumbled and kept quiet.

We had left some stuff behind at the Dorje guest house, where the staff were no doubt eyeing it with terror, thinking that it is possessed by SHE WHO MUST BE OBEYED, and so we had a nice excuse to go back there to reclaim it. Adi also wanted to do some shopping, because he is half a woman. And beer in tea-pot was a strong motivator as well.

CALL YOURSELF ADVENTURERS! I CAW ON YOU! The crow went and shat on our bikes and flew off and exploded, showering the place with feathers and crow.

All of us were silent for a minute and then sheepishly went to pack up. Our 3 Enfields, which normally looked bigger and fiercer than all the other bikes on the road, looked puny in front of the two

BMWs. Indi was riding a 750 cc bike which was so tall that he had to jump up on it like a monkey shinning up a tree, and the planters's 1200 cc BMW was even bigger. Rajesh scowled at his rented Bullet - he was still thinking of his poor dead Norton, which was a powerful 700cc one, and the two stoner boys were blissful on their ancient RD 350s.

'Macha, why don't you try riding my bike?' Indi offered hospitably 'Check it out, see if you like it.'

'No man.' I replied. 'Thanks all the same.'

I never ride anybody else's vehicle, or lech at their wives. What is the point? If theirs is better, then you just feel bad about your property, and if your's is better - then you feel sad for the other guy - that he can't do better even than your own modest lot. Be happy with what you have and lust not after your neighbour's sweet ride, as Moses said.

There was a flapping noise as another crow came and sat on my shoulder, and put his beak close to my startled eye.

YOU HAVE ANYTHING TO SAY?

No no, not at all - I said hurriedly, and wiped my brow as the crow cawed derisively and flew away.

We submitted Khardung la again, and again these buggers took a hundred snaps of themselves in front of that sign, and bought various knick knacks from the Army store, and again I looked bemusedly at the sign that said that an Army team had roller skated up there.

Roller skated up here? Seriously? How does that even work?

It was afternoon by the time we hit the pass and the midday sun had started the snowmelt, and that had swelled the water streams flowing across the road and it was muddy and slushy and much much challenging. But that was only for a few kilometres and soon we were speeding down the mountain road and making our way back to Ladakh.

Soon we were back at Dorje guest house, much to their alarm, and Adi was orgasming with joy as his mobile pinged back to life.

'Oh my beauty, how I had missed you!' MUAH MUAH MUAH He kissed his phone deeply, then looked at it again and licked the screen, and tried to give the charging port a french kiss, and then kissed it again and cradled it in his arms and crooned with happiness.

Dorje was looking at him with disbelief.

'Did he receive a call from his girlfriend?' he asked.

No,no..we replied. He is just happy at getting back into internet range.

In the evening, we went strolling to the market and Adi bought earrings, and nose rings and toe rings for himself, and also some bracelets and bangles. He probably would have bought eyebrow rings and bellybutton rings and nipple rings if we hadn't dragged him away, bitterly complaining.

In the evening we had a tandoori chicken dinner, along with beer in tea pot and went back to the room, where we waited till midnight and then beat up Adi with sticks and stones to celebrate his birthday. We pummelled him and jumped on him and whacked him around the head to wish him a happy birthday.

Its not everybody who gets to celebrate their birthday on a biking trip in Ladakh.

Leh to Pangong lake

After some relaxation in Leh, it was time for our next great destination - Pangong lake - the famous huge mountain lake, and to access this, we would be crossing the second highest motor able road in the world - Chang-la pass.

Woo hoo!

For this journey to start, it was essential for every one to first ... wake up.

And this was a task as usual. We had had a disturbed night, and it was all Adi's fault. If it hadn't been his birthday, then we would not have had to wait till midnight to kick him.

After our midnight exertions, it was a task to wake these guys up. Ordinarily I would have had to work up a hell of a sweat kicking and punching them until they woke up, but this morning I was inspired.
I just knelt down and whispered one word in their ears
'BHARATHI'

And next thing you know, these big lugs are standing, fully packed and geared up next to their bikes, smartly saluting me.

I winked to the sardonically watching crow and set off on our next adventure.

Pangong lake is one of those wonderful mountain lakes which dot the Himalayan plateau - providing huge patches of water in the midst of a mountainous wasteland. We have always been fascinated by these waterbodies, and have always attached semi divine status to them. The most famous example of this is the Manasarovar lake near Mount Kailash. People are so fascinated with these lakes that they are willing to undertake the toughest of pilgrimages to see them. The Kailash pilgrimage used to be so dangerous that people used to perform their last rites before they set out on it.

Unfortunately, most of these lakes are in Tibet, and Tibet has been conquered by the Chinese - and the chinks are definitely not going to allow us to go there to check them out. The Pangong lake is partly in Tibet and partly in India.

The road was the same as the one to Nubra, and so we had breakfast at the same dhaba - the one with the simple paratha and rajma, and the photos of the buxom Sonakshi Sinha adding colour and sex appeal to the walls. That food was so awesome - dhaba food at its best. Simple and delicious.

Then we were off to the next destination - the third highest pass in India - Chang La!

Chang La literally means 'South pass' or 'Pass to the south', and is one of the passes between the ancient kingdom of Tibet and the Indian subcontinent. It is one of the routes of the ancient silk route (though a smaller lower route) that was used to transport high value goods between China and the rest of the world. Now it is tarred and modernised and is supposed to be the second highest motor able pass in the world, at 5360 metres/ 17590 feet above sea level. Of course, if you say this to a geography nerd (cough Bharathi cough) they will jump on you and start biting you and tell you that this is not the case, and there are other passes and bla bla bla..but who cares? We were on a trip and we were happy to be doing the second highest pass after doing the highest motor able road (another red flag to the geography nerds - they keep screaming that K top is not actually the highest motorable road) of Khardung La.

It is to the east of Khardung-la, so you ignore the left turn to Khardung and go on ahead to Kharu and Sekti village. The road was awesome, as the BRO had done a great job till there, and then it got a bit fucked when we started climbing up. The snow clearance and the melt water just scrapes the tarmac off the path and you are climbing up a steep muddy road with streams of melt water across it. The scenery was great and the road was challenging and our powerful bikes were roaring, so we felt good. But the road got steadily worse as we approached the top and one had to be really careful on the steep turns especially as there were giant trucks and SUVs bearing down on us.

Bawa was obviously overjoyed on seeing such a fucked up road and he shouted 'YAHOOWAOAOAO' and zoomed up merrily the road, taking care to hit every rock and gravel and broken road he could. Adi was a little more circumspect and zoomed a little more slowly, while I went up in my measured way, with one eye appreciating the scenery and one eye on the road.

As Adi was neither zooming nor appreciating the scenery, the motorcycle gods sneered at him and splash! He slipped on some mud, wobbled a bit and instead of speeding up to create momentum, he tried to put his foot down for support, couldn't manage that as well, and had a slow and embarrassing fall into the mud. PLOP. He was down on the ground with his bike on top of him.

Bawa didn't even notice, as he was so far ahead. I saw Adi fall, but couldn't see any safe place to stop and so went on ahead. Adi couldn't believe that I was abandoning him. He wriggled on the mud, trying to get up, but his bike was heavy and the thin air at that altitude left him too weak to push the bike off him. At that moment, an SUV full of tourists came by and splashed him with mud.

'Rescued at last!' he thought, but all that happened was that the tourists in the cab squealed 'OOooo a fallen biker..what fun!' and snapped photos of him and went off. They didn't even stop the car, leaving him gazing incredulously at the tail lights of the departing cab.

I found a place to park the bike, and dismounted and went down to help him up, but by then another car had stopped and they had extricated him and pulled the bike up. I assuaged his wounded feelings by laughing loudly at him and slapping him on the back and calling him a 'fallen woman'. We got his bike started and went up and found bawa who was waiting ahead, wondering where we had gone to.

Soon we were at Chang la, the second highest motor able road in the world.

It was a much better place than Khardung-la as there were less tourists, and overall seemed better organised. The Indian army serves free tea up there, and it was very welcome indeed. Long live the Indian army.

There is a Chang la baba temple, dedicated to the god of the pass and like all high passes in the area, it was festooned liberally with Tibetan prayer flags.

It was a glorious and clear day, and the views were fantastic! This was a high pass - the highest in the area - and the mighty Himalayas were all around us. The clear blue sky and snow capped peaks, completely barren of vegetation, made for a truly amazing sight. And obviously there was the obligatory photo session for these two photo whores - photo with helmet in hand, then helmet on hip, helmet on other hip, then helmet on bike, then with arms akimbo, then both of them with hand on each other's shoulders, then both of them kissing (not each other...kissing the signpost) etc etc etc. Then they went and ate Maggi, then bought T shirts and keychains and knick knacks...

'Here boys..' I said 'Hurry up...'
'Oh shut up.' They replied. 'Bloody old fogey. Are we going to come to Chang la again and again? We should enjoy this experience! We are mighty mountain men! We are the great bikers! The world deserves to see our glory..our photos... our virility...'
'Oy virile and hairy person' I interrupted him 'All I say is that we are 5300 metres above sea level and you shouldn't stay too long at this altitude. You might get altitude sickness again and bawa will do a Darang Durung on us again.'
'Oh shit.'
'Shit is right'
"I might be getting a headache' Adi said, patting his helmet with a worried look.
'Altitude sickness can cause cerebral oedema, which can result in death' I observed, and Adi went pale and immediately jumped on bike and zoomed off. 'AAAARRGGHHH'

I grinned and followed them.

Coming down from Chang la, We were entering the Changthang plateau, which is the area between the Great Himalayan range and the Karakorams. It is an incredible place - 'A great cathedral of silence' as Gaurav Jani describes it.

Gaurav is a rider and filmmaker who has made some amazing motorcycle travel films - 2 of which are based on his travels in this area. 'Riding Solo to the top of the world' was his first film about his ride to Changthang, and was one of the things which inspired me to come here. He explored the area in depth, and interacted with the local nomadic people called the Chang Pa. The Chang pa rear herds of Yak and Pashmina goats in the mountains and happily live here where the temperature goes to minus 35 degrees centigrade in the winters. He lived with them in their tents and was so impressed with them that he made another film called 'Motorcycle Chang pa' - which is not released as yet, but I am sure will be great. Gaurav - In case you are reading this - we are waiting eagerly for it.

While it would have been great to do a Gaurav Jani and stay for months and months and be one with nature and shit on the open prairie in minus 35 temperature and stroke yak testicles and whatnot, we had neither the gumption nor the time to do the same. Just the experience of the ride there in the summer was enough for us.

Coming down from the pass, there was a long road of nothingness and it was a long time before we got to a village where we could get something to eat. It was a one horse village and the only place to eat was a small dhaba operated by a matriarch and some younger women - probably daughters and daughter in laws. The menu was the normal mountain menu - Maggi or thukpa. I was sick of the maggi, so I tried the thukpa and that was pretty awful as well.

I wondered a bit about life in these remote villages…what it must be like. It must have been so remote, so cut off from the world till just a few years ago. Then over the last 50 years or so, the army presence has increased a thousand fold, and the tourist traffic as well. But after the summer is over, they are back to their remote and cut off life. No one around for miles, and nothing to do but the daily chores. Must be mind numbingly boring. Keep in mind that these must be the rich and well to do people here - the nomads and villagers would be living a different life altogether - alone in the meadows and wastelands and seeing nothing but their family and yaks for months on end. But I suppose that they are happy and contented, and sneer at us city folk for living such strange and hurried lives in dirty, crowded and polluted cities. Such is life - where everyone is happy sneering at the other guy.

We set off again on the road, and I was looking around and enjoying the feeling when suddenly my bike lost all traction and went swerving around the road, scaring the shit out of me. What the fuck!

Sand!

The bloody mountain road was covered with sand.

I thought we had left the Himalayan desert back in Nubra, but here was some more of it, and like all sand it decided that it would be great fun to spread itself all across the road and scare the shit out of unwary riders.

Bawa and Adi were of course, overjoyed and they went WHEEEE over the sand, while I crawled over it eschewing all risk. Sand is my Kryptonite.

'You should speed across the sand dude,' Bawa said 'That will actually add to your momentum and prevent you from skidding and falling.'

'Yes, I know that mentally' I replied 'But my body overrides me'

We crossed a long sandy stretch and finally came in sight of the mighty Pangong lake.

What a lake it is! Its frikking huge! Its a long snake-like water body, 134 Km long! About 60% of it is in Tibet and rest in Indian territory. The Tibetan plateau is full of giant lakes, but only a few of them are in Indian territory and this is the biggest of them.

It's truly a remarkable sight…you have to see it to appreciate it. It is smack in the middle of the mountains, on a high plateau - about 4500 metres above sea level. There is nothing around - no water no trees, no vegetation - and suddenly you see this ginormous water body - its like an inland sea! And it has salty water, so it doesn't support any life - that explains the lack of greenery, animal life or farming. It's amazing - a salt water sea in the middle of the highest mountain range!

The bright blue sky, the brown and sere mountains, and this emerald green-blue sea - its a world wonder.

The Chinese conquered Tibet in the 60's and so a large part of the lake is in Chinese hands. The Chinese being Chinese, maintain that the whole lake is theirs along with any part of the land that touches the lake. The Indian army says 'screw you' and maintains that this lake is ours and so there is always a state of playing 'chicken' out there, with both armies staring each other down, and this leads to a heavy army presence there.

The Indian government actually promotes tourism here that reason, to show to the world that this is undoubtedly Indian territory and so the army does not interfere with the tourists. This used to be the final frontier of Indian tourism, with only the hardiest and most determined of travellers coming here. But over the years, with the bettering of the roads, it has become more and more accessible and the film makers have descended on it like a bunch of locusts. Some big bollywood films started it, like Dil se, 3 idiots, Jab tak hai jaan etc, and then the ad film makers took over. Now it seems that any bloody ad is shot here - from underwear to motorbikes - and now every bloody tourist wants to hire an Innova and come here and take a photo of himself on the banks of the lake.

The good part of this is that there is a boom in availability of accommodation - something which was worrying me a bit, as we had no idea where we were going to stay, and we obviously had no tents or stuff. It was warm during the day, but it promised to get really cold in the night.

These were mostly tents, which entrepreneurial locals had put up by the lakeside, and we checked out a few of these. Some were cheaply priced, but were pretty sad in quality so we went on to a swankier tent group, which turned out to be pretty nice. It was large Swiss tents, with nice beds and clean linen, and a separate loo tent which also looked clean. And they also had a restaurant where we could get food.

'How much?' I asked him.

'Hmm…' he looked at us thoughtfully, wondering how much he can sting us for. '4000 per head' he said.

'Balls.' I replied. 'I don't want to buy the tent - just to stay in it for a night.'

'No sir…' he tried to defend himself 'look at the quality of our tent…see the location..we also serve food. Just see the place…'

'I am seeing the place…' I replied 'and I am also seeing that it is empty. Better give me a good rate or we will ride on ahead and it will remain empty. Better to make a little money than no money, isn't it?'

And so it went, and finally we got a rate of a thousand bucks for all three of us.

'But this doesn't cover the food!' he said finally, trying to salvage as much as he could.

'OK, no problem - we will pay separately for the food.' I didn't want to cut him to the bone after all. Poor fellow, he also needs to make some money for the effort of putting all this up in such a remote location.

As I was walking off, he came running and plucked my elbow.

'Sir…please don't tell the other guests about the rate we agreed on…they are paying 4000 bucks each…They have come in an Innova with a driver after all.'

We happily entered our attractive tent and pulled off the saddle bags and riding gear, and went off for a ride on the lake front and…you guessed it - a photo session! The two of them with the lake, with the bikes and the lake, with the bike only, jumping up and down, catching a photo of them in the air..etc etc. By the time the photo session was over, the sun was setting and the temperature was dropping sharply and we made our way back to the tents.

That's when the great bearing replacement episode happened.

'Yaar bawa…' Adi said, affectionately placing his hands on Delzad's shoulder '…my front wheel is acting up a bit. Maybe the bearing is getting worn out.'

'Reeeeally?' Bawa straightened up with a jerk, a light glowing in his eyes. 'Bearing acting up? You interest me strangely, my friend!'

'Yes…and I was thinking…if the bearing were to break in the middle of the ride, I would be in trouble.'

'Yes indeed! It would be a problem…the front wheel would start to wobble like Ketan's belly.'

'And in the sand too…' Adi mused. 'So risky with this bearing.'

'It so happens that I am carrying a spare bearing!' Delzad shouted

'You are? My hero!' Adi squealed in delight.

'And all the tools to change the bearing as well!' Delzad started jumping up and down and almost widdled in excitement

'EEEEEEEEEE…..' Adi screamed in joy and they both held hands and started jumping up and down together teenaged girls going to the prom 'EEEEEEEEEE….We are going to change the bearing ….we are going to change the bearing….we are going to change the bearing….'

I was looking at them in disbelief.

'Here…What's going on? What's going on? Knock it off, people are staring at us.'

'We are going to change Adi's bearing.' Delzad announced.

'His bearing?' I was mystified. 'You mean his posture…the way he carries himself? His sexual orientation? Here?'

'NO NO….the bearing in his bike, you idiot, the ball bearing. The tyre rotates on metallic ball bearings, and those are wearing out and need to be changed before they break'

'Oh? I had no idea that my bike had balls. How will you change them?'

'We will remove the front tyre from the bike, then use a special tool to remove the wheel bearing, replace it with the fresh one I have in the bag, and then remount the wheel.'

'What!' I was dumbfounded! 'Remove the wheel? Here? On the shores of Pangong lake - one of most deserted areas in the country? And in the dark? Why? Why now? Why not later? In Leh? Or at least in the morning?'

'NO NO NO' they chorused 'We will do it here. Here and now. Real men do it in the dark.'

'But what the fuck! Why do such a high risk procedure at such a place? What if you drop something and lose it in the dark? What if you are not able to fix the wheel? How will we get the bike back to Leh?'

'This fat guy is such a coward, I tell you.' Del sneered at me.
'Such a loser.' Adi agreed.
'And ignorant as well.'
'And ugly too.'
'Why do you think I carted all these tools all the way here eh?' Del asked. 'I am THE mechanic. I am vishwakarma incarnate. I am Vulcan reborn. I sneer at this puny task. I will do it in precisely 12 minutes. Or less.'
'Have you ever done this before?' I asked him.

'Tchah!' he said royally, and pointed at the setting sun. It was almost on the horizon. 'See that sun? Well, keep seeing it my friend, because I will be through before that sun sets. Come Adi - Let us begin!'

He snapped his fingers, and Adi saluted and they got to work.

The whole thing reminded me of a description of how eminent doctors used to amputate limbs and do operations in the pre-anaesthesia days. The patient would obviously be in tremendous pain and so the main skill of the doctor was how fast he could do the operation.

'Time me, gentlemen…time me' the doctor would say and get to work with a hacksaw or whatever and the blood starts flowing and the screaming starts.

Similarly, Del said 'Time me, gentlemen, time me' and got to work on removing the wheel and hey presto - it was off in minutes. They looked at me triumphantly, but I was impassive. I have always found it easier to take stuff off rather than put it back.

He quickly replaced the bearing, and started putting the wheel back.

'Hmm' He was puzzled and tried again.
And again.
And again.
And again.

'Whats up?' I asked. I was sitting far away, as they didn't trust me with tools and stuff.

'Nothing. Nothing.' He replied and tried again.

And again
And again.

The problem was getting the brake pads to stay in place. They kept falling out whenever he tried to replace the wheel and hanging out. It was like a surgeon who has removed the kidney, but the liver keeps falling into his hands when he tries to close the wound.

Adi was nothing more than a mechanics mate here, as his mech skills were far below bawas, but he also tried his luck and failed.

The sun had long set now, and it was pitch dark and still these two were struggling with it, like 2 Sisyphus's pushing their rocks up the hill, only to see it rolling down just as they had got it to the top. They were sweating inspite of the cold now, and were streaked with oil and grease and very pissed indeed.

There was weeping and wailing and gnashing of teeth. Tears were welling up and lips were being bitten; savage oaths were bubbling in bosoms and the slightest provocation would have resulted in violence and bloodletting. Delzad's hair were standing straight up, and Adi's cheeks were bulging because his balls were in his mouth.

I didn't say a word, as firstly they would probably had attacked me with a tyre iron, and secondly as I was also worried as to how to get the one legged bike back to Leh. Chances of a mechanic here were quite remote, but we had met a biker group and they might be having a mechanic with them. Else we would have to look for a truck going back to Leh...

While they tried and saw that bloody brake pad fall.

Again
And again
And yet again.

They became a tourist attraction by themselves out there…the tent operator and his staff came to watch - they found it so fascinating that they made tea and came to watch, the tourists in the adjoining tent came and offered to put on the lights of the car so that we would have some light. They made some popcorn and we sat around and watched a powerful human drama of emotion and action. Big Boss had nothing on this stuff.

We would probably be there still, if not for the driver of the Innova who was compelled by professional curiosity to come and help us. He first came and squatted next to us to observe, then he started to point and give advice, then he moved in to hold stuff and push and pull, then he finally shooed both of them off and got really down and dirty with the tyre and showed it who's boss, and finally shoved the pads in and glared at the tyre until it got too afraid to push it out again, and they quickly pushed the wheel back and locked it in, and stood there gasping.

They were tired and irritated and covered in oil and grease. It was dark and cold, and a cold breeze had started to blow. When we went inside to eat, there was no non-veg either to raise the spirits. Even the rum was over.

'Well Adi' I said as we were getting to bed. 'Your thirties have certainly started off with a bang, I must say. You have changed your bearing at Pangong lake. You have become a motorcycle Chang Pa yourself'

'True dat man.'

'Should have recorded that on film - we could have called it 'Changing bearing solo on top of the world' and scoffed at Gaurav Jani. You wimp - you may have changed punctured tyres, but we have changed wheel bearings.'

We bumped fists and went to sleep.

Pangong to Leh

The next day dawned clear on Pangong lake, and we emerged from the tent to gaze on the beauty of the lake. It was really an awesome sight. That blue aquamarine water, framed by the brown bare Himalayan peaks, and that brilliant blue sky…godlike stuff.

And Adi takes one look and again goes to his bike, squats down and starts peering at the oil level.
'Yaar bawa…do you think my oil is low? Do you think we should drain the sump and fill fresh oil? Do you think we should change the gear sprockets? Do you think we should do open heart surgery on the bike here, as it is possibly the worst place to do such a thing and therefore would be a great and stimulating challenge to your mechanical skills? Do you think we should change the handlebars? Do you…OUCH'
He finally stopped babbling and clutched his ass where I had kicked him, and sulked.

'Lets move out of here before he starts dismantling his bike himself.' I said to Delzad, and he agreed. His fingers were still black and sore from his nights ordeal and he went pale at the thought of doing something like that again.

We had breakfast and went to pack up, and soon the usual cry was heard.
'Guys…I can't find my glares!'
Me and bawa looked at each other and rolled our eyes.
'The goggle killer is at it again.'
'What number is it now?'
'18, I think'
'Oh, I thought it might be more.'

Adi came out complaining 'Why are you guys just sitting there? Help me find my sunglasses.'

'I told you to buy a box of them.' I said

'Oh shut up. I am sure you only must have hidden them.'

We loaded our saddlebags on the bikes and put on our riding gear, but Adi still couldn't find his glasses.

'Never mind now, just add it to the list of the departed and buy a few new pairs in Leh.'

'What nonsense, I will take a look again and see'

He was feeling too lazy to walk up to the tent, so he decided to go on his bike itself, and soon the inevitable sound was heard.

CRACK.

'Ah. Looks like he found it.' I said, and bawa nodded.

Adi came back, looking shamefaced as usual.

'Well…what happened? Stepped on it again?'

'You guys keep exaggerating! I don't always step on my glasses! And for your information, I did not step on my glasses.' He said with dignity, tilting his beard up loftily.

'Then what was that crack?'

'I…er…accidentally rode my bike over it…I didn't see it on the ground, and only heard the sound of the crack.'

'Ah…' we nodded understandingly.

'…It wasn't my fault…it was hidden in the grass…'

'19 now?' I asked bawa and he nodded.

'Oh fuck you.' And we mounted up and rode out of Pangong and headed back to Leh.

The hill near Lukung is apparently known as 'Garnet hill' and these semi precious stones were apparently lying around for the taking all over it. By now most of the garnets must be picked up already, but some are apparently still to be found on top of it, where we also could have gone and filled our pockets and saddlebags with it.

There were a few problems with that idea though - one was that the whole place is full of hills and we would have had no idea as to which is the garnet hill. Secondly, we wouldn't know what a garnet is, and what it looks like and probably have picked up each and every stone except a garnet. And thirdly, the army people might have come and kicked our butts all the way back to Leh.

All this was a moot point anyway - Mr Perpetual motion was gone long before I could enlighten him about garnet hill.

The same applied to Durbuk gompa and trying to spot the rare black necked cranes which apparently come to Pangong lake to breed and whatever else was worth seeing around there. Adi would just sit on the bike and twist the throttle and be gone, and if bawa saw a rough patch of road, he would scream with joy and vanish, and I would just sigh and ride behind.

This perpetual motion thing nearly got us into trouble with the cops too.

There is a check point after Chang la (or before - depending on which direction you are going) where you are supposed to register your bike and show ID and stuff, but while coming up, Mr P.M. Had just ignored the waiting guard and zoomed right by, and we had followed as well.

The guard simply waited as he knew we had to come back on the same route. We actually made his job much easier by actually stopping near him and asking road directions. He chewed us out for not following rules and threatened to keep us here all day to punish us, but Adi burst into tears and begged for forgiveness — BOOHOOHOO...how can I stay in one place, I have to keep moving..BOOHOOHOO. The guard was so taken aback that he let us go, and was probably glad to see the back of us.

We crossed quite a few monasteries on the way back - monasteries at Chemrey, Stakna, Thikse and Shey - and we saw none of these! Just passed them by. The main reason was that the two Amigos were not interested at all, and were only into the perpetual motion concept, and I was also not fanatical about seeing them.

To be honest, they are kind of repetitive - one big buddha, thangkas and paintings, etc. If you have seen one, you have seen them all.

'BLOODY PHILISTINE' a thought burnt into my skull.

Ah - She Who Must Be Obeyed is back in range I see.

We went back to Dorje guest house, much to Dorje's horror, and parked ourself in his rooms.

We spent the evening chilling out in Leh and doing touristy stuff like buying T shirts and knick knacks and stuff and had dinner with the Bangalore boys. Their dreams of doing the adventurous routes like the Agham Shyok road and Marsimik La and whatnot had all come to nought - much like I expected they would. They had wimped out and quietly come back to Leh.

Later we heard the sad story of Indi and gang's denouement of their Ladakh trip. The fancy bikes all broke down. The Norton had died on Zoji La and the BMWs died after Nubra valley and had to go back ignominiously in trucks, and the bikers had to go home shamefacedly in a flight from Leh. The only bikes which survived the trip was the Royal Enfield and the two ancient RD 350s. In fact the Harold and Kumar pair rode all the way back from Ladakh to Bangalore on their RD 350s and ganja clouds. That is the reality of touring in India - the roads are so fucked up, that the fancy bikes just can't take it, and once they crock up its impossible to get it repaired. Enfields fall in the sweet spot of being tough enough to take the fucked up roads, powerful enough to clip at a reasonable pace on the good roads, light enough to pick up and push, cheap enough not to worry about it being a total loss, can be loaded in trains, ships and trucks and are somewhat repairable across India. All they need is to have better quality control so that they don't break down and leave you cursing at the side of the road.

Siddharth Lal - hope you are reading this. Improve the frikkin' product quality.

The next day was a rest day, where we would just chill and do all pending chores.

Our Leh chapter was over -now we were off to Tso Moriri and the Leh Manali road.

Leh to Tso Moriri

'UTHO REY…UTHO…UTHO…CAW CAW CAW CAW CAW CAW…'

The usual siren song ran through our heads and jerked us awake, along with all the guests and staff of Dorje guest house. Today the call was more strident, probably because she had been unable to get through to us on the Pangong Too trip and all her energy was built up. The crow was already smoking and sparks emanated from the tips of its feathers. Tendrils of electricity ran from it to all corners of the house, making Adi's beard sizzle and Delzad's tight curls furl and unfurl. The leftover electricity went into the wires and all Dorje's lights came on with unearthly brilliance and started exploding as they couldn't handle the charge of She Who Must Be Obeyed.

'Stop stop…' poor Dorje whispered from below 'Please utho rey…my house will explode…I beg you, utho rey…'

'All right, all right' I mumbled as I woke up and rubbed my eyes, and Adi slapped his face to stop the sparking. Del just opened one eye and went back to sleep, spooning Adi affectionately, but his own hair tried to strangle him and he woke up with a jerk.

'Whats all the panic? We are utho-ing.'

TODAY IS THE DAY WHEN YOU LAZY SODS HAVE TO DO SOME REAL MOUNTAIN RIDING AGAIN. HAHAH AH. HOPE THE FLESHPOTS OF LEH HAVE NOT MADE YOU SOFT.

She was right - we were leaving Leh behind, and heading out on some real rough roads. We were heading to Tso Moriri lake. We would head South east towards the Manali highway, and turn off at Upshi where we would follow the Indus river to the village of Chumathang, which is famous for hot springs. There is a 'hot spring resort' there, where apparently the enterprising hotel guy has built a resort right on top of the springs, so that you have to stay there to soak in the springs.

From there we would carry on to the Mahe bridge, where we would cross the Indus and carry on to village of Sumdo, where there is a small gompa. And from Sumdo, it would be 48 km of unpaved, raw roads past the village of Puga, and then cross the high pass of Namshang La at an altitude of 4800 metres, and then enter the lake area - first there would be small lake of Tso Thang, and then we would come to the magic lake of Tso Moriri.

All this travel would be along roads which could be pretty rough, and there were no petrol pumps and very little population. The total distance would be about 211 KM, and after the turnoff at Upshi, the road quality would be very suspect indeed.

We were planning to spend the night at Tso Moriri and in true Amigos style, we had no bookings and no plans, but trusted to the god of idiots to find a place to sleep.

From Tso Moriri, we planned to loop to the near by Tso Kar lake and from there join the Leh Manali highway at Debring, thus craftily avoiding the high pass of Tanglangla and cutting down the driving distance by avoiding a large loop of the road. We were so smart, I tell you.

The Leh Manali road was obviously a hard ride by itself - it is 500 KM of insane riding across 4 high passes - Tanglang La, Lachulung La, Baralacha la and Rohtang la. This is the dream ride of most Enfielders, indeed of all bikers, and they get aroused and start ejaculating helplessly just at the thought of it.

But for us, since we had done that crazy Zanskar ride, and of course Khardung la and Chang la already, we were looking at it with much less awe. It would be much less hardcore than the other roads, as it is a very important road for the military and thus is kept in good condition. Having said that, it is a kickass ride and we would be stretched indeed to do this itinerary all the way to Manali.

Thus the insane cackling from She Who Must Be Obeyed, we were indeed embarking on a rough few days of hard riding.

HURRY UP HURRY UP HURRY UP! HIT THE ROADS EARLY! YOU ARE IN THE HIMALAYAS, NOT IN THE SAHYADRIS!

'All right, all right…keep your feathers on' I said, and we packed up and left. All the members of Dorjes's family and his guests were hiding under their beds until we left and once we kick started and rode off with a mighty thump, we could hear everybody cheering and shouting 'Hip Hip hurrah!' and dancing and throwing confetti around. But then the crow went back and landed on a window sill, and again everything went silent as they all dived under the beds again.

We hit that same road again and again passed Shey, Thikse, Stakna and Kharu and continued straight down the Manali highway. I sighed a bit as we passed all these places, it would be cool to stay in Leh for a couple of weeks and explore all the area around at a leisurely pace. It was my third visit to Leh and I still felt that I had not even scratched the surface of the place. I will come sometime later and do this - do some trekking and cycling as well. There are so many wonderful treks in this area, and so much to explore. And of course, in different seasons the landscape totally changes. I had seen photos of Leh in the winter and it looks like a different world altogether. The whole of Pangong lake freezes over! Can you imagine that? Being a shore dwelling softie, my balls would freeze solid as well and make a clanking noise when I walk - but I would love to experience it. One guy I know did the 'fat bike expedition' where 3 cyclists installed fat snow tyres on their bicycles and cycled this whole path in the dead of winter!

Sigh. So much to do.

But for now, we were motorbiking! And it was great fun too.

We followed the highway till Upshi, and then turned off on to the Rupshu trail, so called because it enters the Rupshu area, which is the name for the plateau and valley in that area, and is the area of the Chang Pa nomads.
The road immediately deteriorated and became a dirt track and we were bumping around on it. We had thoughtfully packed some petrol because there are no petrol pumps in that area.

Adi rides a Classic 500 which has a petrol tank the size of a thimble - about 12 litres. Only Royal Enfield can design a touring bike which has a testicle sized tank and no fuel indicator, so you will have no idea when you will run out of petrol and be stranded on a lonely highway. You can tell a Classic owner by the way he keeps opening his petrol tank and peering into it or shaking his bike and listening carefully to the sloshing sound like a doctor without a stethoscope.
Me and Del had our wonderful Thunderbird 500s which are much better designed for touring. The seating position is superb, the

tank is a hefty 20 litres and it has a digital petrol gauge - it doesn't work half the time, but at least it is there.

Anyway, Adi's puny tank meant that he was hyper sensitive about petrol and had filled all the bottles he could find and stuffed his Ladakh carrier full of it, and then persuaded bawa to carry another 2 litre bottle in his saddle bag. Unfortunately, the road was so bumpy that the 2 litre bottle just jumped out and dropped off somewhere, presumably to be discovered someday by some lucky fellow.

Adi was shattered when he found out
'OOOOOOO....THE BOTTLE HAS GONE.....WHAT WILL I DOOOOOOOO....I WILL BE STRANDED HERE AND DIE ALONE.....OOOOOOOOOOO'
'Here, stop that!' I hissed. 'People are staring. Anyway why are you so bothered, you are carrying enough petrol to fuel yourself.'
'BUT MY BOTTLE....BOOOHOOOOHOOO'
'Shhh' I hissed. We were standing in line to show the police dude our inner line permit and I noticed him looking sharply at us, checking for possible insanity. We were still a little scarred from the threats of that earlier checkpoint guy and didn't want to take any unnecessary risks.

We cleared that silly checkpoint with those pointless inner line permits (Now ILPs are no longer required for this region thankfully. But if you are planning to go further to Dah and Hanu villages, you will need them) and carried on along the Indus towards Chumathang.

The road was wild and rocky and the scenery was awesome, and so I was riding slowly and going crosseyed by the need to keep one eye on the road and the other on the scenery. Bawa obviously was enjoying himself tremendously on the bad roads and was going WAHOO and zooming along and scaring all other motorists.

But after some time, he disappeared! I crossed Adi and we rode together for sometime and wondered where he was. Normally he would zoom ahead, but then wait for us to catch up somewhere - but now he was nowhere to be seen.

We reached Chumathang village, of hot spring fame, and stopped there for lunch. It was the default lunch stop as there were no other villages on that route, and all the bikers and motorists were there. But still no sign of bawa, or his bike.

Strange. Should have met him by now.

Me and Adi decided to have lunch while waiting, and had some grub at the dhaba, and was wondering whether it would be a good idea to have a soak in the hot spring out there. But I decided against it - hot springs are chancy stuff, and the sulphur fumes can fuck up your head sometimes and make you dizzy and disoriented. Not a good idea when there was quite a bit of riding still to be done. But it would be amazing if you are planning to chill out and stay the night. There wasn't anything to see or do apart from the springs, as it was pretty much a one horse town, but if you are taking it easy then it would be a great idea. Especially if you are cycling or horse riding, it would be a great break in the middle of a trip.

But since we were doing neither, we sat tight and quietly ate and drank and waited for bawa.

But no sign of him. Strange.

I asked around the various hotels if they had seen him, and finally one guy said that yes - such a bike had gone on ahead. Cursing a bit, we went ahead but all we could see was an empty road.

I was wondering if he had fallen into a ditch or something, or maybe been kidnapped by a horny chang pa or the sinister communist army, when we saw him.

He had parked his bike and gone to sleep! That fellow can sleep anywhere and at anytime. He was waiting for us and decided to have a nap rather than just stand there. Which does make sense, I suppose.

We stopped and woke him up with a swift kick on his backside, and we carried on.

The next waypoint was the Mahe bridge, where we cross the Indus. The straight road goes on to Tibet / China and the turnoff is a fucked up unsurfaced track which goes to Tso Moriri. In fact, it was so bad, that we didn't realise that it was a road at all, and went merrily on our way on the better road.

After some time I started feeling uneasy…surely there was a turnoff which we should have taken…strangely low traffic on this road…started feeling a bit odd. After some time I stopped and signalled the others to stop as well, and turned around.

We came a little ways back till the turnoff and looked around doubtfully. I saw a couple of army guys in the distance and went off to ask them for directions.
'Sir, is this the way to Tso Moriri ?'

He looked at me quizzically and said 'No…that is the road' pointing towards the unsurfaced road.

'Oh…I see..' Now I noticed that there was a small dilapidated sign pointing it out. 'Oh dear, we went down the wrong road for some time then.'

By now the guy had looked us over and decided that we were harmless, so he smiled at me and said 'Yes I know. If you had gone a bit further we would have shot you…you are only a few kilometres from the China border. If we hadn't shot you, the Chinese would have.'

Adi went pale and shot off on the correct road like a bullet….hmmm…unfortunate analogy.

This road was truly horrible, and a real taste of offloading so we thoroughly enjoyed it. Its amazing, if we had been in a car or bus, we would have been miserable, but since we were on our bikes we thoroughly enjoyed it. Its great fun to gun your bike on a smooth road and take steep bends and scrape your foot pegs, and it is equally good fun to tackle a truly fucked road and power your way through it. You are on full alert, and looking out for loose stones, gravel and pot holes which are the obstacles, and looking out for the easier patch of road where you can get through. And of course, the challenge of maintaining a decent speed all through. It's like playing a game with the elements.

After about 50 KM of this challenging road, when finally we saw the lovely blue waters of a lake, and we YOOHOOed with joy. We had made it! We were at Tso Moriri! YES!

We stopped by the lake and took selfies and photographs and were generally kicked with life, until I noticed that this lake was rather small - smaller than expected. Granted that it is smaller than Pangong, but this much smaller? And also it was totally deserted - there was no one and nothing around. How strange. I had heard that there were hotels and buildings and stuff around.

We were standing there and looking when another guy came and parked behind us and came out to take a look.

'This isn't Tso Moriri, you know.' He said suddenly.

'Say what?'

'Yes…this is that smaller lake that come before Tso Moriri - Tso Thadsang.'

Oh! Well, we withdraw the YOOHOO then. But it was really beautiful. That aquamarine lake in the middle of the bare plateau looked really amazing under that clear blue sky.

Ah! That sky. What can I say about that highland sky? It was a clear sky, and bright blue and seemed much larger than any sky can be. One state in US is called the 'Big sky country' and I know exactly what they mean. This is the kind of sky that makes travelling worthwhile.

It was a wrench leaving that place, but we were moving towards an even better place. And practically speaking, it was nearing evening and we had to clear security there and look for a place to stay as well.

There was an Indo Tibetan Border Police guy sitting there to check our Inner Line Permits and keep a copy for himself…we had been warned that we should have a lot of copies of that stupid ILP to hand over to all the security checkpoints and so we had contributed to the local economy of Leh by taking a number expensive photocopies.

Some other tourists were in a jam, because the lady did not have extra copies of her ILP, only the original.

'Sorry madam - you cannot stay here unless you give me a copy.'

'But I don't have another copy...but I have the original- you can see that.'

'I need a copy for my records.'

'Er...OK, then you keep this original then.'

'Then you will be caught at the next check point, and I will be in trouble because they will think that I let you pass without checking your papers.'

'But you have my papers!'

'But they won't know that.'

'But what can I do then?'

'Get a copy made.'

'Where can I get a copy made?'

'In Leh.'

'Leh! How can I get to Leh? Its dark and I want to stay here!'

'Sorry, but I need a copy....'

I went off shaking my head. What idiocy. Wonder how they sorted it out in the end...that policeman looked like a single track minded fellow who was determined the follow the rules, come what may.

Tso Moriri itself was a disappointment, though. They had walled off the access to the lake as it has been designated as a national park or protected area or something, so we couldn't go close to the lake. In these areas close to border, it is a very bad idea to try and clamber over fences as the army is on high alert at all times and practises a 'shoot first ask later' doctrine.

Accommodation, as in the case of Pangong, turned out to be fairly easy to get, as there is quite a bit of tourism infrastructure built up there now. There are resorts, and tented camps and home stays galore. We found a nice tent for us, and paid a premium price for it because it had a view of the lake. This turned out to be a really stupid thing, because that view lasted for only about half an hour, after the sun set it became completely dark. Lake view or wall view, it would have been the same to us.

I was hoping for a beautiful sky view, because this would be among the least polluted places in the world and the night sky would be amazing. Unfortunately, it turned out cloudy and overcast and we couldn't see a thing. Inky black lake merged with an inky black sky and that was about it as far as views went.

Bummer.

Instead of the magical star gazing evening which I had in mind, we stayed inside the tent and watched movies on my mobile phone.

But hey - it was the journey which mattered more than the destination. And the journey had been quite wonderful. So no worries.

Tso Moriri to Sarchu

The next morning we bid adieu to Tso Moriri, and started out for the next lake of Tso Kar. This itinerary was a bit rushed, I felt - maybe one should plan to spend more time at each of these lake fronts - but I think they might get a bit boring after a few hours. Also Tso Moriri was so fenced up and surrounded by dangerous looking security people that it might not be a nice experience.

There was a gompa at Korzok, but we didn't get around to seeing that either. It's an unusual gompa because it is staffed and run by nuns rather than monks, so it would be probably better run and better maintained than all the other one, but we missed it…the perpetual motion thing…

Maybe the trick would be to ride a little faster and reach the lake earlier in the day, so that you can enjoy the lake views without adding a day to your schedule. But then you would be having time pressure on your riding time.

The road to Tso Kar was similar to the road to Tso Moriri - raw and unmetalled, and we were doing real off road riding all through. Bawa andAdi were extremely happy and screaming and smiling like fools and flying along, while I was a slow and careful and plodding along. I was like a turtle behind two jackrabbits.

We had met a german motorcycling tour group at Tso Moriri - they were an interesting bunch. They seemed to be all seniors - probably 60 plus, retirees, white haired, wrinkly types, and had come to India for the first time. The touring company had organised the Enfields for them, so they were riding those bikes for the first time - that too in Ladakh. Hell, for all I know, they might have ridden a motorcycle for the first time on this trip.

And each and every one of these decrepit old fogeys on borrowed Enfields came from behind me and overtook me and left me eating their dust! Finally the support vehicle - a lumbering huge van carrying the mechanic and sundry spare parts and tyres and stuff also came and grinned at me and overtook me and left.

I felt like the slowest turtle on earth at that point. Slooooooooow. Pathetic. Loser.

But the views were simply amazing, and I was enjoying the ride, so why worry? Its about 70 Km from lake to lake, and that landscape was like nothing you will ever see anywhere else.

Its possible that these two lakes were part of the same great lake at one point, and over the centuries the waters have evaporated and these two are the remnants of the old large water body. While the land looks bare and lifeless, there are groups of black necked cranes and Tibetan wild asses out there, and so the whole area is designated as the Tso Kar wildlife sanctuary

The only wild asses I saw were the Amigos and I finally came to Tso Kar, and these two were waiting for me. They seemed to have been waiting for so long, that spiders had made cobwebs all over them.

We had breakfast at a dhaba overlooking the lake. The lake is pretty nice - its surrounded by wetlands and marshes, and is a favourite spot for waterbirds like Brahminy Ducks and Grebes as a stopping point on their long migrations.

The interesting thing about Tso Kar is that it is much saltier than the neighbouring Tso Moriri - so salty that the local Chang Pa use it as a salt pan and harvest the salt and sell it in the mountains to the monasteries and villagers in Tibet and ladakh. In the ancient days, the traders used to take tea and salt to the hills and come back with pashmina wool, and herbs and sometimes gold and precious stones

Now of course, since iodised salt is freely available, this is not done much.

We set out from Tso Kar, and soon our lake loop was over. We would soon be joining the Leh Manali highway and would be back in traffic and civilisation.

Now here was where intelligent planning and route creation comes in. If you take the Leh Manali road, you have to pass through 4 high passes - Tanglang La, Lachulung La, Nakee la and Baralacha La - all of whom are pretty high and challenging passes. These can get pretty nasty weather at times - clouds, snow, rain etc and can be a royal pain.

Now, by cutting into the highway from Tso Kar, we would very smartly be cutting into the highway after Tanglang La and would thus avoid a long retracing of the route and avoid a high pass as well.

Bharathi had planned this out, of course, and before we left she told us umpteen times - 'Remember - Debring' …'Remember Debring' …. 'Hit the effing highway at Debring, you effing twits!' …. 'LEFT…take LEFT'

Even at Tso Kar, I had noticed a Yak plodding towards us with a grim expression and mooing 'DEB…RING…MOOO…..DEB…RING…MOOO'

'OK guys' I said to them 'Remember that we have to take the turn to Manali at Debring. Any questions?'

They snapped to attention, clicked their heels, saluted briskly and said 'Aye Aye sir! No questions sir.'

We got on to the bikes and vroomed off. I was sad to leave the wild and untrammelled atmosphere of Tso Kar, but it would be nice to get on to proper tarmac roads too. We reached a tarmac road after some time and the traffic too increased. Clearly we were on the right track.

The god of roads has it in for me, and wherever I go, he punishes me with dug up roads. Whether it is Mumbai or Bangkok or New York or the Australian outback, I will always get stuck in dug up roads. It is a curse and cross to bear.

Thus, I was not really surprised when we ran slam bang into road construction. The dust of the roads, the diesel fumes of the generators, the smoke and tar smell from the melting tar pots, the exhaust fumes from the vehicles all hit us all of a sudden and disoriented me a bit, and we reacted in the typical way an urban biker would - we zigged and we zagged and overtook and cut traffic as much as we could in our urge to get past the traffic choke point.

Adi is in his element when it comes to traffic - on a clear empty highway he will drive at a measured speed, but when he sees a crowded road he goes crazy - he will take both hands off the handlebars and stretch, speed up, zig and zag like a drunken moth - I think his ambition would be to do a handstand on the saddle and steer the bike with his beard, while riding on a really crowded road.

And so here also he was off like the Flash.

I was grimly manoeuvring my way through traffic and wondering when that blasted highway was going to come, and bawa was contentedly following me. We fought our way through stones and sand and tar melting points and labourers wielding sledgehammers and pickaxes, and trucks and tempos and army vehicles, private cars, bikes and clouds of choking dust and grimly continued onwards.

I stopped to ask a worker where was the route to the highway, and he confidently pointed ahead and we also carried on ahead. Suddenly the road construction ceased, and the road became better and emboldened by this, Bawa suddenly decided 'fuck this shit' and zoomed ahead, and I streaked behind in pursuit. Adi must be far ahead, I thought, and we must catch up with him.

A long time passed, and no sign of Adi.

'Bloody irresponsible fellow!' I thought. 'Bloody young hooligan! Whippersnapper! Twerp! Abandoner! Blackguard! He should have stopped and waited for us. Wait till I catch up with him…I will give him a piece of my mind!'

Another long time passed. Still no Adi.

Strange.

But we kept zooming along.

Suddenly we came to a yellow sign in the road, and I braked to take a look at it.

I took a look at it.

Shit!

The sign said 'Tanglang La' !

We had been going in the wrong direction! We had totally missed the turn at Debring and were riding back to Leh!

Shit! Shit! Shit!

Luckily bawa had not gone zooming ahead as usual. He was waiting impatiently a little way ahead, wondering why this fat fool was fooling around taking photographs of stupid road signs when we had such a long distance to cover. I signalled him to come over, and at first he refused, and came only when I gestured again and again.

'What is it?' he asked angrily. I just pointed to the sign.
'What are you pointing at signs for? Even I can see the sign. Tanglang la..so what? Lets go!' He was in a state of road hypnosis. I just looked at him, and he registered it after a few moments.
'Shit! Tanglang La!! Why are we here? We were supposed to be avoiding Tanglang La!'

HEH HEH HEH. A rumbling laugh sounded in our heads. YOU CANNOT GO WITHOUT SALUTING ME, YOU MISERABLE MORTALS.

'Whodafuck? Whadafuck?' Bawa nearly jumped off the bike and started shivering and quaking

I AM TANGLANG LA. I CALLED YOU HERE TO SEE MY GLORY. HAHAHA.

'Oh…I see…er…nice to have met you sir, hehehehe…' We stammered and saluted the post. 'Er…can we take your leave now?'

There was no answer, and passers by looked at us with surprise, two bulky bikers saluting a road sign and talking into thin air. A bus stopped and disgorged a horde of photographers wielding huge cameras and lenses and started snapping us. One guy prostrated himself in front of us and I thought that he is saluting us out of respect for our biking achievements - but no, he was just trying to get an unusual angle for a photo.

Bawa shrugged philosophically and posed happily for them, and then took out his camera and started taking pictures of his own.
'Hey' I said urgently 'Why are you wasting time taking photos?!! We have come the wrong way - we need to go back down!'
'Chill yaar.' He drawled. 'Baba Tanglang la has called us all the way here, we might as well enjoy the place for a minute and take photos. Looks like we were destined to do all the high passes, whether we want to or not.'

I thought about it for a minute and agreed. Why not? I also got off my bike and we sat there for a few minutes, enjoying the beauty of Tanglang pass, more than 5000 metres above sea level, and one of the highest passes in the world.

It would have been a shame to have missed it.

We turned the bike around and went zooming down the road - which we now knew to be the Leh Manali highway - and came past the road construction area and then saw that the settlement of Debring was just beyond the point of the road construction. There was a turnoff at Debring, and there were a group of tented hotels and dhabas at that point, which we had missed entirely. Adi must have taken this turning, and we missed it.

'Might as well have a cup of tea here.' Delzad suggested, and I agreed.

As we were standing there, a biker stopped and asked us 'Are you Aditya's friends?'

Wow. We were famous. Or Adi was famous. A guy we don't know from Adam is asking us if we are Aditya's friends.

'Er…yes..we are. And you are…?' I asked.
'He is waiting for you down the road at Pang. He asked me to tell you if I see you.'
'Oh, that's great.' I said 'That's a load off my mind - we were wondering where he has got to.'
'But how did he know that you will be the person to find us?' Delzad asked curiously.
'Oh - I think he has told every biker he could find. Two guys on Thunderbird 500s - one with yellow helmet, one with black helmet…please tell them that Aditya is waiting for them.'

And that was true. Every bloody fellow we met on the way down would slow down and ask 'Are you Aditya's friends?' Finally we would reply even before the biker could open his mouth 'Yes we are. Thanks a lot. Bye' and leave the bikers in awe of our awesome ESP. The legends of the mind reading bikers is still going around in Leh, and they are considering building a gompa to us I believe.

But the most interesting thing was to happen now. We finished our tea and were just about to mount the bikes, when a group of bikers came up and asked piteously if we had an air pump. He had had a puncture - they had a mechanic with them who changed the tube, but they didn't have a pump to fill air in it. That biker was screwed big time - a flat tire, a pillion, Tanglang la yet to be climbed and the nearest repair shop a very long way off.

Air pump? No… I replied. Adi was carrying the pump.

'Wait a minute…wait a minute.' Bawa said suddenly. 'He was complaining about poor weight distribution, and so he put the pump into my saddle bag just today morning. We do have a pump.'

That biker's face lit up like a lightbulb.

Bawa rummaged in his saddlebag and fished out an electric air pump, hooked it up to his battery, and inflated that guys tyre. That biker was so happy, his trip had been narrowly saved from disaster. He thanked us from the bottom of his heart.

'I asked so many people on the way, but you were the only people who had a pump with them.'

'When did you get this puncture?' bawa asked.
'About an hour ago.' He replied.

Me and bawa looked at each other and smiled. This biker was incredibly lucky. If we had followed the right path, we would have been well beyond Pang by now, and this guy would have not met us and got his air filled. He would have been screwed.

Looks like God made us do this long detour just so that we could help this biker in distress.

And indeed, that was the only time that pump worked. We tried using it once later, but it refused to work ever again. It was destined only to help that stranger - I never asked his name, and don't remember a single thing about him now.

We came down the road without issue and came down some beautiful twisty turns to the small settlement of Pang, where a most distraught Adi was waiting for us. He was weeping and wailing and covered in dust, and looked like the maiden wailing for her demon lover. He had almost torn out his beard in grief and looked like a sloth bear with a secret sorrow.

'OOOOOO…WHY DID YOU LEAVE ME….WHY WHY WHY…BOO HOO HOOO'

'Here, relax.' I said, with a glance about us 'People are staring at us.'

'OOOOO BAWA….I FELT SO LOST WITHOUT YOUUUUUU'

Bawa also was consumed by emotion and got off his bike and went near him and whacked him on the head.

'OW'

'Idiot! Why didn't you wait for us at the turn like a lead rider should?'

'Eh?' Adi was taken aback.

'Yeah' I chimed in, realising that offence was the best form of defence 'Why didn't you wait at the trail marker? Because of you we went all the way to Tanglang la. Its all your fault!'

'Yes, its his fault'

'What nonsense!' Adi was incensed. 'There is only one turn on the entire bloody road! How could I know that you will miss that one turn? Are you blind?'

'One turn or many' I said firmly 'turn is turn. You should have waited for us. Its all your fault.'

'But...'

'No buts!' Bawa agreed with me 'Your fault it is. As a punishment you will buy the booze once we hit Manali.'

'But...I sent word through every biker I could find. I have been waiting here for hours!' Adi wailed. 'I was so worried!'

'That is also your fault.' I said 'Every bloody biker was stopping and giving the same message. You are the first spammer on the Leh Manali highway. Your penalty is to buy drinks twice now.'

'But...'

It was getting pretty late now, and I wanted to cover as much road as possible today. We planned to reach Sarchu tonight, so that we could hit Manali the next day and keep on schedule.

We left Pang and enjoyed the ride on the smooth tarmac of the Moray plains. The first time I had come to Leh, there was no road on the plains - you just drove on the raw land itself. But now they have made a magnificent smooth road on the plains and you can enjoy a fast ride. While it was very nice, it detracts from the Moray plains experience a bit. And indeed, Bawa went off the road and decided to enjoy the ride off the road.

We crossed two high passes - Lachulung La and Nakee la. Lachulung La is above 5000 meters and is a seriously high pass, and has the worst road conditions of all the passes. Its a disgusting road full of craters and sand and road hazards, and was all the harder for being unexpected. Nakee La is about 4700 meters and is quite unremarkable - you wouldn't really notice it if not for the sign and the prayer flags. We stopped at both passes to take photos and pay our respects. After the Tanglang La experience, I was determined not to offend any pass god.

And after this we went on to one of the most anticipated parts of the trip - the Gata loops! These are 22 hair pin bends where we descend sharply down 500 metres in a very short stretch of road. We had been looking forward to this for days, but now it was getting dark already and we would have to rush through the loops.

We started on the loops in high spirits, looking to do some steep turns and scrape our foot pegs as we leant at a steep angle to the roads. But as we started I felt a presence behind us, and in the mirror I saw a huge truck right behind us. It looked dark and ominous - it hadn't switched on its lights and even the engine was off - it was utterly silent and coming down on gravity alone. The steep Gata loops gave it plenty of gravity and the truck came behind us like a hungry least, eager to hunt and devour us. Trucks have long been used as a means to murder in India - a truck can knock over a vehicle and crush even a sturdy four wheeler - a bike would simply be flattened like a cockroach!

We gunned our bikes and made a run for it, but the phantom truck was hard on our heels! Normally a truck is easy to spot due to the noise and heat and vibrations of the engine, and the bright lights; but this was like a dark and noiseless menace - an evil presence. We ran like the hobbits running from the ringwraiths.

'Even though I walk through the valley of the shadow of death, I fear no evil for you are with me. Your rod and your staff comfort me'

We were riding with fear through the loops of the shadow of death, and my rod was completely shrivelled up and provided no comfort at all.

Finally we found a bit of lay-by and scrambled into it and lay panting, as the truck zoomed by silently in the dark. Safe! Safe at last! The killer has missed us! WooHoo! WE ARE ALIIIVEEE!

Now that the danger was past, we could appreciate and admire the skill of the truck driver to take all 22 loops on momentum alone, without any help from the engine. But by goom - that was scary!

'Shit yaar...' Adi said sadly, looking back at the loops. 'I was scared that I didn't get to enjoy riding the loops. Lets go back up and come down again.'

A tempting idea, but it was dark already and soon would be very cold indeed. But at least we had done the loops in record time.

We had planned to go all the way to Sarchu, but it was almost pitch dark and I was looking for a place to stay. We checked out some dhabas and finally decided to stay in a shady dormitory tent. It was the simplest accommodation one could ask for - just a tent and a bed. The hotel owner also had a small kitchen where he served food and chai. The rent was extremely modest - a hundred rupees per person.

What more could one ask for?

We were on the mid point of the Manali Leh highway. Tomorrow we would reach Manali and the hardcore part of the ride would be over.

We toasted our ride with some rum, it had been a most eventful day, and inspite of a couple of hiccups - a most enjoyable day.

A day to live for.

May there be many such days.

Sarchu to Manali

We got up early and enjoyed the pleasures of an open air crap in freezing cold weather.

There is nothing quite like the experience of taking a dump in the open - the fresh air, the cool breeze playing on your bum, the dawn sky blushing at the sight of you all hanging out …Even washing up with ice cold water is a refreshing experience and instantly removes all thoughts of sleep from your mind. Much more effective than washing your face.

We returned energised, and had breakfast and started off. Today was a big day - the last day of the Leh highway ride - we would be crossing 2 huge passes - Baralacha La at 5000 Meters and Rohtang La at about 4000 meters.

Baralacha used to be a really tough crossing, as it is heavily snowbound. Even now, with the BRO using heavy machinery to keep it clear, it is quite an imposing sight with walls of ice on both sides. The meltwater from the glaciers creating rivers of icy cold melt water going across the road and creating challenging water crossings for vehicles.

On the way to Baralacha, we crossed some pretty fancy swiss tent hotels - if we had gone just a little further last night, we could have stayed in comfort here. The place looked pretty empty, so I am sure we could have bargained a good rate. But I was happy we stayed in that spartan dorm tent - it was more in keeping with the ethos of the Leh Manali ride.

There were quite a few water crossings where the meltwater flowed, but since it was early in the day the ice had not fully melted yet and so the streams were quite shallow and we could cross them with ease.

It is quite unpleasant to get your feet wet in these crossings, as the socks can't dry out inside the shoes and you are cold and miserable through the ride and your toes wrinkle up like raisins. As these streams were still shallow, we were able to pass through with dry feet.

It is a different story when you are coming from Manali, as you would be reaching Baralacha later in the day and so the place would be a watery mess. Add to that the fact that this would be the first day of your highway ride, and you would be already tired from crossing the mess of Rohtang pass - this would mean that you would be seriously pooped by the time you cross Baralacha.

THATS WHY I COMMANDED YOU TO DO SRINAGAR LEH FIRST, YOU INSIGNIFICANT IGNORANT WRETCH.

Oh goody. She was back in range.

The road rose a bit and became mountainous and wilder as we approached the high pass of Baralacha. There was ice and snow everywhere, and the road was muddy and watery. But it was amazingly beautiful - there were a couple of meltwater lakes at the side of the road, and the water was a deep blue azure. These mountain lakes are all wonderful, especially in the arid Himalayas, where they really stand out in the brown surroundings.

This was the Suraj tal - a glacial meltwater lake which is the starting point of the Bhaga river, which combines with the Chandra river to form the Chandrabhaga river, which is a famous river in Indian folklore.

As per legend, Chandra was the daughter of the moon god and Bhaga was the son of the Sun god. For some reason, they decided to go to the top of the Baralacha and run in opposite directions. As Chandra was a woman and therefore far more sensible, she easily found her way to Tandi and waited for her man. Bhaga was probably feeling all macho and shit and struggled his way through some tough gorges and finally made his way huffing and puffing and all muddy to Tandi, where they finally met and no doubt Chandra snickered at him derisively and said that he was too stupid to face life alone and needed a woman to take of him and Bhaga was too tired to run away; so they got hitched and became the Chandrabhaga river.

WHY ARE YOU RUINING A PERFECTLY GOOD LEGEND BY INTERJECTING YOUR LIFE STORY IN IT?

Well why not? Life imitates art, art imitates life and all that.

Baralacha apparently means 'Summit with Crossroads' in the local lingo, and this was the place where paths to Ladakh, Spiti, Lahaul and Zanskar met in the ancient trade routes. Not on top of the pass of course, but in the general area. This is the pass where you move from the green Himalayas to the brown Himalayas. Or vice versa. Depending on what direction you are going. We were now exiting the Tibetan plateau and entering the alpine Himalayas.

But first was the salute to Baralacha. We stopped at the top and saluted the pass and took some photos. The scenery was mind blowing.

In talking about a trip in this area one really runs out of words to say and I can just imagine the reader saying 'yeah yeah, we get it. It was mind blowing, awesome, whatever'. But it really is.

You are at the top of the world and looking around at the greatest of God's creations. That is the reason you have put your body and your bike through so much torture. This is the reason we love our Enfields - because they can take you to see such spots.

Sure, you can go in a nice comfortable car, with the heater on, and music playing and eating snacks and drinking soft drinks. But that is pointless. The real joy is in doing this trip on a two wheeler, where you can actually feel the place, the weather, the winds, the temperature, the challenge of the road.

Four wheels move the body, but two wheels move the soul.

YOU WIMP.

Me a wimp? Why?

THE TWO WHEELS YOU SHOULD BE DOING IT ON IS A BICYCLE! USE YOUR OWN STRENGTH TO CLIMB, NOT A BIG FAT ENGINE.

Ah. Er. Um.

HAH. TCHAH. HMPHH.

Ah, well - maybe we will do that too someday. As of now, I am happy to be doing it on my Royal Enfield. I soaked in the scenery for a bit more, and tried to check out the three valleys of the Chandra, the Bhaga and the Yunan, and then leaving the pass behind, started the descent to Zingzingbar.

The scenery was amazing going down - the vegetation was spare, but the valley was like an artist's imagination running riot. Deep crimson, grey green, indigo, mauve, lilac and a dozen other brilliant colours.

We came down this beautiful place and stopped at Darcha, where we had to register with the police. This sounds impressive, but it actually means writing your name and number in a tatty little register. God alone knows what use this is.
'If someone goes missing, then we can search in this register to see if he has passed this way' the cop explained to me when I asked him. Sounds like a damn silly idea to me - but I suppose it gives someone something to do.

From Darcha we passed Jispa and Keylong. Keylong is the entry to the Lahaul Spiti region, and is supposed to be quite a cool place as well. Its supposed to have a nice market and restaurants and hotels, and you can park yourself here while you explore some interesting temples, gompas, forts, lakes and treks around it.

Obviously, with Mr Perpetual Motion in action, we didn't see any of this and carried on to Tandi. The most interesting thing about Tandi is that it has a petrol pump. Why should a petrol pump be interesting? Because it is the only petrol pump in 350 Km! They are very proud of the fact and have a big board on top that says so.

After Tandi, the road was very scenic as we were going along the banks of the Chandra river. We passed the very pleasant villages of Gondla and Sissu and Khoksar, until we were staring up the last of the grand passes of the route - the famous Rohtang pass!

To most people, Rohtang pass has come to signify a pleasant picnic spot. It's a day excursion from Manali, and you can hire rubber boots and warm clothes from the many stalls on the way up from Manali, and go there and play in the snow and take photos. You eat Maggi noodles and drink tea and watch the garishly clad honeymooners simper for photos. The macho wannabes go around bare chested to show that they don't mind the cold at all, and go running up the slopes and come sliding down in inflated tyre tubes. There is always a filthy traffic jam on the way to the pass, and the whole vibe of the place is like a fairground.

A non-serious, playful place is what most people think of it.

But the history of the place is very different. The very name 'Rohtang' means 'pile of dead bodies'. WTF. What an ominous name.

This is because the pass was so treacherous that hordes of people died while trying to cross it. It is a pass across the steep Pir Panjal range, and served as a trade route between people living on either side of the Pir Panjal. It is a clear dividing point - between the Hindu culture of the Beas valley and the Buddhist culture of the Chandra and Chenab basins.

The ascent from Koksar to Rohtang is very tough, because the road is always in poor condition due to the snow and rain and meltwater, and is a mess of mud and gravel and stones. We were now inured to bad roads and were not particularly fazed by the sight of the road.

Just then we saw a huge group of bikers coming along the pass. It was the Himalayan Odyssey! The Royal Enfield company runs a few bike tours to encourage people to go on long rides and get a taste of the touring life. They organise the route, the stay, the permissions, maintenance back up, mechanic and spare parts and stuff and you just pay some money and ride along. The Himalayan Odyssey was the first tour they started, and it is still their signature tour -the one they are most proud about. It is also their biggest group - with 50 to 70 riders plus the support vehicles.

It is an excellent way to get introduced to touring - my first long ride was with the Royal Enfield Tour of NH17, where we explored the Bombay Goa highway. I have done RE tours to Rajasthan and Nepal as well and I would recommend it unreservedly - especially for beginners.

But there was no fucking way I was getting trapped behind 50 beginners on the ascent to Rohtang! I would die of frustration. All three of us had the same idea, and we gunned our bikes and zoomed up the cliff!

Just at that point, the leaders of the Odyssey - the representatives from Royal Enfield - also decided to test their mettle against the climb and they also gunned their bikes and Vroomed up the path and it was now a race!

The adrenaline rush was incredible as we ascended the pass at an amazing pace! Mud, slush, stones, slippery patches - we disregarded all of them as we just trusted our machines, our tyres and our riding skill. I would never ever have climbed up that path as smoothly and effortlessly as this if I had done it in the traditional conservative way. If we had gone slowly, the heavy bike would have got stuck in the mud, slipped in the slush or stalled somewhere. But since we were maintaining high speed and acceleration, the momentum of the bike ensured that we had a smooth ride up.

I have never enjoyed an ascent as much as that, it was something amazing! That ride up Rohtang removed all the tiredness from us and left happy, energised and excited. We parked at the top and saluted the Rohtang top and took some photos as we allowed the bikes to cool off. It was crowded and messy but it was OK. We had completed all the major passes of the ride, and now the ride was pretty much over. Everything would be downhill now. We hugged each other and thumped on backs - we had done it.

The scenery changed abruptly as we came down - the mountains on this side of the pass were green and verdant and full of life. We followed the Beas river down and it was lovely as a picture postcard! After so many days in the brown and bare scenery of Ladakh, this was like entering a beautiful garden. The roads were in excellent condition and butter smooth, and it was amazing fun to bend into the curves and enjoy a fast and smooth descent.

There were forests of Pine and Deodhar on the mountainside, lush green pastures in the valley, the river was burbling and gurgling over its rocky pebbly bottom, and people were enjoying adventure activities like river rafting and para gliding. The whole feel was so happy and joyful, that I was singing in my helmet. Even my voice sounds wonderful when it reverberates in my helmet.

We stopped at a beautiful riverside restaurant for a cup of tea, and then carried on to Manali.

Manali is a very ancient town - it was the beginning of the ancient trade route to Ladakh, and from there to the Karakoram pass and on to central Asia. The name 'Manali' is supposedly derived from 'Manu-alaya' - which means the abode of Manu, who was the sole survivor of an ancient deluge - A Hindu version of Noah and his ark. He had been warned by Lord Vishnu that the world was going to be drowned in a huge flood and so he built a boat and filled it with animals and stuff and enjoyed a relaxing cruise until the floodwaters abated and he found himself stranded on a mountain somewhere and probably scratched his head and wondered what the fuck to do now.

It used to be a very nice place - I had been here as a kid in early 1980's - very quiet and non commercial. The tourists used to go to Kashmir or Simla which was bigger, had more and better things to see and had much better tourism infrastructure. But then Kashmir shut down in the 90s due to the terrorism problem and all the tourist crowd shifted to Manali. Manali wasn't geared up for so much tourism and got swamped and it became a huge mess. But over the years things have settled down, tourism infrastructure got built up, measures were taken to save the ecology and now its better than it used to be.

The last time I had been to Manali, I had come with Bharathi and we had stayed at Vashisht, near the ancient hot springs and had enjoyed it immensely. The vibe of the place was much more chilled and relaxed than the busy Manali town, and it was a place for foreign backpackers rather than Indian family tourists.

We made our way to Vashisht - its up quite a steep hill and we made quite a racket going up the slope. The roads got narrower as we got near the old temple and hot springs area, and we stopped near a fancy looking newly built hotel right on the cliff edge. The owner was a businesslike guy and he immediately showed us his fanciest room - it was a lovely top floor room with a lovely view through a huge french window, wooden floor and panelling and even a fireplace.

The hotelier quoted a fancy fee, but came down very sharply when I pointed out that we seemed to be the only guests around and it was better to get less money than no money. We closed the deal and went upwards and stripped off the riding gear and relaxed.

Such is life - last night we were in a spartan tent and shat in the open, and the next day we are in this very fancy room.

I had very fond memories of Vashisht hot springs from my last visit with Bharathi. We had done that trip on public transport - rattly state transport buses and were a bit stiff and sore from our trip through Lahul Spiti region and Rohtang pass, and so were glad to try out the hot spring. That water was so hot that it almost parboiled my balls, but it was incredibly relaxing and was a lovely experience on that trip, so I was keen to try it out again.

Adi and Del were not much into the idea - they didn't have any experience of hot springs, and the idea of a public bath was a bit weird for them.

'How can you take a bath with other people dude?' Adi asked doubtfully, plucking his beard in thought.

'Its not like a communal shower, idiot.' I responded 'It's like a heated swimming pool. No nudity - so you don't have to worry about bumping hairy danglies with others.'

They were still unconvinced but when they saw how enthu I was, they agreed to come over and take look.

The bath was somehow not as nice as I remembered. Either I had been looking at the memories with rose tinted glasses due to the romantic nature of that first trip with She-Who-Must-Be-Obeyed, or the maintenance of the place had taken a dive. It looked dirty and dingy, and like all sulphur springs, it stank a bit.

I jumped in anyway, but these two wimped out and ran off. I soaked for a bit and then came out - it wasn't as nice as last time. Sigh - never repeat a place - it always is a downer.

These two had gone shopping for knick knacks, and I was chatting with the hotel owner while waiting for them.

'So how's business?' I asked, and he shook his head mournfully. Business was very slow, he said.

'The last guest in your room was a week ago, but he was here for a week or two.'

'That long eh?' I asked.

'And he hardly came out of his room! I thought that he was going to starve to death.'

'Eh? What was he doing? Meditating ?'

'No no…he was smoking up.'

'Smoking?' sounded funny to me. 'How many cigarettes can a guy smoke?'

He gave me a pitying look, as one would give to a village bumpkin or a very innocent kid at a burlesque bar. 'Not tobacco sir…hash…charas…'

'Oh!' Oh right…Manali is the home of Malana hash, supposedly the best hash in the world.

'I would like to try some too!' I said, and he looked at me even more pityingly.

'Have you ever tried it before?'

'Er…sometimes…but only a puff from someone else…I don't know what to do with it.'

He puffed out his cheeks and looked at me, apparently wondering if it was worth the risk to help out such a bumpkin, and then said Ok - he would send someone over.

Then these two came back, and we went out for dinner and I forgot all about the conversation. Then in the evening one guy came to the room, bowing and smiling.

'Heh heh…hello sir…the manager sent me…you wanted something…'

'Oh yeah…that thing…wait a sec.' I told these two, and they were immediately excited.

'OOOOO yes…Let's get stoned!' Adi said with glee, rubbing his hands together.

'OOOOO yes…Lets toke up!' Del said, rubbing his hands together.

Big talk from people who can't even roll a joint. We were complete amateurs, and all the stuff used to dribble out of the joint even before you could smoke it.

'Ok then, let's go with this guy.' I said.

'Go? Go where?' Adi asked

'To the dealer.

'OMG! Visit a drug dealer! What if the guy turns out to be a mafioso and kidnaps us? What if the cops raid and find us there and jail us? What if a deranged addict attacks us and kills us and drinks our blood? OOOOOO….what if we all die here? What will happen to my bike ?Who will take care of her…OOOOOO…' Adi started wailing in grief.

'Here…relax.' I hissed, 'That guy will run off. You stay here, Me and Del will go and pick it up.'

So we nodded to the guy and went with him into the village area, and to a little house.

It was quite a trippy scene when we entered the house. There was a psychedelic radium picture of Shiva smoking a chillum on the wall, and all the lights were dim. There were a bunch of people seated around in a circle, who were passing a chillum around like acolytes in some religious cult. The guru in the centre was the dealer, and there was a bunch of firangs around him. The sickly sweet smell of hash percolated in the air and there was some sitar music playing in the background.

We nodded at everyone, and everyone greeted us and we took our place in the circle and took a puff when the chillum came to us. Whoof! That was some good shit! It gave me an instant kick and I became all mellow. We sat around in that circle for some time, making small talk and passing the chill around, and finally the hotel guy and the dealer had some chitchat and the four of us went to an upstairs room.

Normally one would assume that a deal of this sort is short and brusque - the dealer would want to complete the transaction as soon as possible and fuck off before the cops came nosing around or that you found out that you have received some useless dried leaves or cowdung instead of the drugs that you paid through your nose for. But this guy seemed to be in no hurry at all.

We had some more joints and some general chitchat. Where are you from? How was your trip? What do you do ? ....cocktail party chat.

'I operate in Manali in summer and in Goa in the winter' he informed us. 'I even have people in Mumbai - you just call me and let me know what you want, and it will be delivered to you.'

'Really?' I asked in surprise 'Delivered?'

'Yes...don't say the name of the stuff. Just ask for atta (flour) or chawal (rice) and we will understand.'

It would be hilarious if one got his number mixed up with the actual atta supplier and you ended up with 5 kilos of marijuana instead of wheat flour. Or vice versa - call up the grocer and ask him for 10 grams of wheat flour.

Maybe he was trying to figure out if we were legit or undercover cops or something, but then he must have realised that no cop could be so stupid and clueless as us, so he reached under his mattress and pulled out a cake of what looked like dried cow shit and tossed it to me. I caught it and looked at it.

'Whats this?'

'Hash - of course.' He sounded slightly indignant. 'The best quality Malana hash.'

I sniffed it and it did smell nice and funky. I had no idea at all as to how to measure the quality of hash, so I just nodded approvingly.

And instead of paying him and walking out I started babbling and asking all kinds of stupid questions. How it is made, and how the business works and how he felt about it and all kinds of crap. Bawa started twitching with nervousness and sweating a bit. After a while he leaned over and whispered 'Lets go man - its been 45 minutes.'

'Right' I said 'OK then - bye.' I said, pocketed the hash and started for the door. I reached the door and saw that no one had moved, and they were all looking at me incredulously.
'What?' I looked down to see if my fly was open or something.
The dealer looked at the hotel guy, and the hotel guy looked at me for a second, then cleared his throat nervously and said 'er…sir…the money?'
Shit. I had forgotten to pay the guy, and was cooly walking out with a pocketful of the stuff!
'Oh sorry!' I said, and paid him and then we walked back to the hotel, with bawa perspiring freely in spite of the cold.

When we got back to the hotel, Adi was nervously pacing up and down so much that he had worn a trail on the floor.
'Where the fuck were you guys? It's been hours! I thought you have been murdered or arrested or something!'
'Ask this fucker' Del nods at me. 'First he chats with him for hours and then walks out without paying.'

Manali to Kalka and back home

CAW CAW CAW …coff coff CAW CAW …coff off

I woke up to the sound of an asthmatic crow, trying desperately to wake us up.

'Whats up? Not well?' I asked

BLOODY CROW'S GOT A COLD. (wheeze) WAKE UP. TRIP IS NOT OVER YET. (wheeze)

Adi opened one eye, saw the crow and jumped up in alarm.

WAKE UP YOU LAZY PODS…ER…SODS…THERE IS STILL A LONG HARD RIDE LEFT! IT'S THE MOST DANGEROUS RIDE YET. CAW CAW. COFF. COFF

Well that's true. The most accidents always happen on the last day of a tour. That's when riders are tired and looking forward to the end of the ride and don't pay the required attention to the road. Also, you are getting back to the high traffic roads, full of homicidal truckers and are not used to such dangers after riding for so long on deserted roads. You need to get focus back to looking at the road rather than looking around at the scenery.

We decided to get a bite of breakfast near the hotel before setting out - it was a beautiful riverside location. It was early in the morning and the hotel staff was still waking up and yawning and scratching their balls; so we decided to go to a neighbouring place where presumably they had finished their ablutions and washed their hands.

The restaurant was on the first floor, and commanded a nice view of the river, and a tourist was sitting there, contemplating the river and the mountains. She was a pretty little white girl, and she looked utterly happy and peaceful. She must have been thinking deep and beautiful thoughts - about life, and love, and god, and creation - and looked calm and serene. Her trip to India must have been her high point in life till then - she would have been patting herself on the back for having made such brilliant decisions to take a break year and find herself and eat, pray, love and all that. The river, the stillness, the crisp air of the morning, the holiness in the air…

Which made what happened next to be really unfortunate.

I had been building up a gigantic fart since last night, and was feeling more like a balloon than a human being - my bowels were distended like a Zeppelin. And possibly because the beauty and serenity of the place relaxed my mind and soul, my sphincter relaxed as well and all the methane and hydrogen sulphide and assorted intestinal gases rushed for freedom, and burst through with a most tremendous explosion.

KABOOOOOOM!!!! That fart was like a nuclear bomb! A megafart!

The noise echoed through the valley like a cannon shot, and sent all the natives scurrying for safety. It knocked the Amigos sideways and the kitchen staff dived for cover, sure that the cooking gas cylinder must have burst, causing death and destruction.

That poor girl happened to be leaning back in her chair at that time, and she was so shocked that she screamed and overbalanced completely and fell over backwards with a crash and the chair broke into pieces, leaving her lying on the floor in the wreckage with her legs over her head, as if she was doing some complicated yoga pose. She went blank in the head and red in the face and gibbered and babbled from the shock. She must have developed a severe case of PTSD and probably required extensive therapy to get over the shock. Poor girl - my heart went out to her, and for that matter, to the two white faced and trembling Amigos as well.

Kabooooom!!! Now the fart echoes bounced back from the mountain like return fire from enemy troops.

The echoes were still coming back from the mountains as we walked in elaborate casualness, whistling jauntily and pretending as if we hadn't even heard any noise. The wooden structure of the hotel gradually stopped rattling as we sat down and peered at the menu, and ordered breakfast from the wide eyed waiters, who gradually dared to come up for air and see what the hell had happened. We pretended that we had not heard anything at all, and the girl was anyway catatonic with shock, so the waiters went away shrugging their shoulders and blaming the noise on a giant landslide in the Himalayas. Or fresh shelling from the army.

After a studiedly quiet breakfast, we went readied the bikes, suited up and bumped fists. This was it. The last day of riding.

'Ride safe folks.' I cautioned 'This will be a tough ride.'

And by jove it was. It was OK for the first part - we crossed the towns of Naggar and Kullu and the roads were quite good and the scenery was still nice. But later the traffic became quite terrible, and you had to really focus. We crossed a mountain road which was on an industrial area, and the truck traffic was extremely thick. All of them seemed to stoned and having a particular grudge against bikers.

I had three near-death experiences on that ride.

One was when we were on the ghats and traffic was moving at a crisp speed. I am pretty conservative when I ride, so I was riding sedately behind a bus and matching its speed and keeping a safe distance, when suddenly a bus driver saw his favourite dhaba and braked hard right in the middle of the road without any warning. SCREEECH. The truck behind him was scared out of his wits and braked hard to prevent crashing into him SCREECH. The bus behind him also shat his his pants and stomped on the brakes. SCREEECH. And I was behind that truck! Buses and trucks have vacuum braking and have huge amounts of stopping power. Two wheeler have drum and disk braking and much less stopping power, and the two wheeler skids and veers when sudden braking is applied. I also hit the front and rear brakes SCREECH and fishtailed wildly and almost crashed but managed to stop inches from the bus - and shocked out of my wits! That was really close - I could easily have crashed into the bus, or slipped and fallen into traffic, or the guy behind me might not have been able to brake in time - all of which would have been fatal.

I cursed and growled a good deal, but there was nothing to be done. I rode even more slowly on the road, but when I was taking a turn, an oncoming trucker suddenly decided to overtake the truck in front of him and swerved unexpectedly into my place, thundering straight into my face. SHIT SHIT SHIT SHIT I screamed and nearly shat my pants! I was banking on a turn and had very little leeway to get out of the way, and the truck missed me by inches. I could literally smell the engine as it passed my me. WHAT THE FUCK IS WRONG WITH YOU? I screamed, but the trucker was long gone.

Fuck this shit, I decided - the problem was that since I was sick behind this bus, I was unsighted and couldn't see what was coming. I decided to overtake the bus and be in the lead - and just as I overtook the bus, a Scorpio also decided to overtake and BOOM both of us were in the same lane, looking with shocked eyes at each other. This time it was entirely my fault, as I was overtaking - and my whole life flashed before my eyes. This was sure death. I would be flattened like a pancake and crushed into mince.

Miraculously the road expanded just enough and we managed to miss each other by a hair. Adi was right behind me and saw it happen and almost shat right there.

I stopped at the lay-by and took off my helmet and wiped my brow. Phew. That was close. My chest was hammering and I was sweating. Whoof.

Adi stopped beside me.

'Dude - that was close.' Adi said after a minute. 'I was screaming into my helmet. I thought you were a goner for sure.'

'I know - right? Fuck me with a wiper blade.'

We relaxed for a while and let the palpitation ease and let the blood pressure come back to normal, and Delzad also joined us, and then we hit the road again. Its important to hit the road as soon as you are OK, else the scare can set in and prevent you from riding. Get back into the ride while you are still warm mentally and there will be no problem.

It was a long ride - 300 km on a crowded mountainous road can be quite a ride, but thankfully it was pretty uneventful after that, and it was getting dark by the time we made our way to Kalka station. Kalka is a small station ahead of Chandigad, and that was the actual starting point of the train. Hence SHE had specifically instructed us to go to Kalka and not to Chandigad, as it would be easier to load the bikes in the train at the starting station.

I was a bit nervous about the time, and hoping that the Kalka railway parcel office would not be closed by then, but it was open and quite bustling as they seemed to have quite a bit of cargo to load. The railway parcel clerk told us that that he was still busy, and that we should come back by 8 PM. That suited us, as we could find a nearby hotel and remove our riding gear and saddlebags and get the bikes ready for transport.

We reached back at the given time and found some local porters to pack up our bikes and after a bit of a struggle, got the bikes packed and registered for freight. The train was to leave the next day, and the parcel clerk assured us that the bikes would be loaded on the train in the morning. So - all systems cleared for take off. We went back to the hotel and had our last dinner on the road. It was a poky little room, and Kalka was hot and muggy, but it was all good. It was the last day of the trip.

The next morning I and Delzad went to the railway station to check that our bikes had actually been loaded on the train, and there was a bit of a twist in the tale. The railway guys had got some unexpected freight to be sent on that train to Mumbai and so only two bikes could be loaded out of the three. They loaded my bike and Del's bike, but not Adi's bike because Adi had fixed that hideous metal Ladakh carrier to his bike which jutted out from both sides and occupied more space than 3 bikes. Adi's bike was standing forlornly alone on the platform.

'What the hell dude?' I protested. 'When will you send the third bike then?'

'Tomorrow' he promised. He would send it tomorrow.

I was most doubtful about this - why would be load the the bike tomorrow if there was no one sitting on his head here? But there was nothing to be done - the luggage compartment was clearly full, and we had a flight to catch in the afternoon. I took that clerk's mobile number and his boss's mobile number and the land line number to keep in touch, and they assured me that there would be no problem and that the bike would be loaded the next day without fail.

I had an idea - the man on the spot would be the owner of the hotel that we were staying in. We had met him in the morning, and he struck me as a smart local guy. I met him and told him about the situation, and asked him if he could follow up with the station the next day to ensure that Adi's bike gets loaded.

He agreed, and asked if we would like to take his taxi to go to Chandigad airport? The cost would be a thousand bucks.

Sure, sure - we agreed. We would take his taxi ,and he would ensure our loading. Quid pro quo. We needed a taxi anyway, so why not take this one.

We told Adi about his bike being left behind only after we cleared security, because that was the only way we could prevent him from rushing to the station and wailing for his bike. Once in the security hold, he would not be allowed to leave, so it would be safe to tell him the news here.

As it is, he let loose a heart breaking cry at the airport, startling all and sundry.

'OOOOOOOO…..MY POOR BABY….LEFT BEHIND ALL ALONE…..OOOOO….YOU HEARTLESS BEASTS…HOW COULD YOU BE SO CRUEL? ….OOOOO'

We carried him moaning and sobbing into the airplane.

We landed at Mumbai and collected our bags and shook hands and went our separate ways.

The ride was over. We would no longer be waking up to a command from SHE - (Well, I would, obviously. But not these two guys). We would not be hearing the musical 'crunch' of Adi planting a size 11 boot on a pair of sunglasses. We would not have to wake up Del from power naps or drag him away from a tandoori chicken.

And we would not be readying our bikes every day and kicking the engine into action and feel the bike vibrate and hear the thump - We would not be seeing those vistas and mountains and that amazing blue sky…we would not feel the breeze rushing through the helmet - we would not see the mountains go past. We would not be taking tight turns on winding mountain roads and we would not be eating at dhabas and meeting fellow bikers and travellers.

But - as they say - 'the party ain't over till the dishes are washed and the table is wiped down and everything is cleaned up'….we still had to collect the bikes and liberate them from the clutches of Indian Railways and bring them home.

Firstly, we had to complete the loading before we worry about the unloading. Adi's bike was still waiting at Kalka station.
As I suspected, it was not a simple thing for Adi's bike to be loaded in the train and it turned out to be a good thing that we had

the hotel owner on our side. He went to the station the next day and found that Adi's bike was still standing there, and had not been loaded yet. I called the parcel clerk and his boss and gave them a mixture of a piece of my mind and abject grovelling, and the hotel guy took it as a special project to protect his given word of honour, and finally they loaded Adi's bike on the train. Without all that follow up, it might have remained there forever.

I didn't dare to tell Adi about all this, of course, as his beard would immediately have gone grey and then he would have wailed and sobbed and pulled out that grey beard in grief. But it turned out all right in the end, so it turned out to be 'Much Adi about nothing'.

The next day I and Del went to the station to pick up our bikes.

We reached the station and showed the parcel clerk our receipts and stuff, but he refused to entertain us until we got an OK from the Octroi authorities.

Octroi - for those who don't know - is an antiquated tax levied by the city of Mumbai on stuff that comes into it. Its supposedly for stuff for sale in Mumbai, and is not applicable on importing your own stuff, but the local guys will always threaten to levy tax and demand bribes for not levying tax. They can be real scumbags.

We went to the octroi people - they had a small office in a repurposed container box - and gave them the papers. Since I was a Mumbai resident and the bike was locally registered they could not charge Octroi. They tried all the same, but I just sneered at them and spoke to them in Marathi and they dropped the demand and stamped me through.

But when they saw that Del's bike had a Thane registration, they smiled wolfishly, rubbed their palms together and made a demand of octroi - as it was a Thane bike entering Mumbai. They fully expected to get a nice bribe out of us, but they reckoned without Bawa turning into Bawasura - the Demon Bawa!

In the course of his factory work, he deals a lot with these insect officials who infest government offices and swarm around collecting bribes - Excise, sales tax, octroi, electricity board, municipality, income tax, service tax and whatnot, and he hates these corrupt people. He was not intimidated by sarkaari officialdom and bureaucratic double-talk and blasted into them with both barrels. BOOM BOOM! I tried to smile and be polite, but bawa was like - fuck that! He got so indignant, that he seemed to swell in size, and his hair coiled and uncoiled like Medusa's locks, and he went purple in the face.

'WHAT NONSENSE!' he screamed 'HOW DARE YOU LEVY OCTROI ON A PERSONAL VEHICLE? DO YOU THINK I AM A FOOL? DO YOU KNOW ANYTHING ABOUT THE ACTUAL RULES? YOU SHOULD BE ASHAMED OF YOURSELF!'

The tax guys were completely shell shocked by the attack and cowered before this righteous indignation and stamped the papers as fast as their hands could move. Normally people plead and grovel with them inspite of being in the right and this frontal assault completely unnerved them. They must have felt like they are being roared at by a man-eating tiger! They went white and grey and trembled before him.

I was fascinated! It was like Bharathi being there!

We went past the trembling Octroi people and plonked our papers in front of the parcel clerk.

'Now you have to get police clearance' that parcel clerk drawled without even raising his eyes from his newspaper, pushing another paper at us. 'Go and look for the police guy, he must be somewhere...EEK' he squealed as Bawa caught hold of him by the collar and jerked him forward, and shook him like a rat and glared at him with bloodshot eyes. Bawa was still fulminating with indignation from the Octroi encounter and that guy shrivelled before his righteous wrath.

'Ah...never mind...my mistake...here are your papers (stamp stamp) - just show this to the policeman on duty one you collect your bike. Heheheh...could you release me now....thank you...heh heh'

Then we went to the platform and hunted out our bikes from all the myriad crap that was strewn all over the place. It was the most disorganised thing, the signage and marking was hopeless, and if you didn't know what you were looking for it would be impossible to find. If we had sent some third party to collect the bikes, he would be there still.

We ripped off all the sackcloth and packaging from our bikes, and wheeled them to the end of the platform, and then went off to find the policeman to get his sign-off. He also came oiling forward expecting a bribe or baksheesh, but he took one look at the still-steaming Bawa and ran off in terror. We had carried a little petrol with us, enough to get us to a petrol pump. A quick fill up at the pump and we rode home in triumph.

The next day Adi went to collect his bike, and he was supposed to come to my place so that we could celebrate the end of the ride in style. He had no trouble with the Octroi, but the policeman got very suspicious looking at his beard and long hair and insisted on checking every nook and cranny of his bike for drugs when he realised that the bike had come from Chandigad and Manali.

'He checked in the petrol tank, in the air filter, in the exhaust pipe, in the instrument box, everywhere.' Adi complained 'He did everything but give me a rectal exam!'

'Ah, you should just have given him your winning smile re.' I said
'Yes, your natural sexual magnetism would have done the job' Del said.
'Fuck you.'

We poured out the rum. We were home, the bikes were home - now the ride was officially over. Everyone was back to their daily life, and were feeling a bit blue. The grind of daily life was back - the work, the boss, the office, the colleagues, the horrendous traffic and pollution.

'Well, now I am back to the cubicle.' Adi said glumly.

'Well, I am back to the factory.' Del said glumly.

'Well, this sofa is very comfortable.' I said. I worked from home after all.

They gave me a dirty look.

'But never mind - if your daily job was not so boring, then you wouldn't enjoy the trip at all. The whole fun of a Ride is how different it is from your daily life. The more boring your normal life is, the more amazing your Ride will be.

So, if you are bored and frustrated, then you are on the right track. Work, make money, get bored - RIDE - work, make money, get bored - RIDE - that should be the rhythm of life. '

'Here's to Boredom!' we clinked our glasses. 'And to the Ride.'

We sipped our drinks and sat quietly for some time, and my thoughts went back again to the ride, to the mountains, the blue sky, the breeze, the thump of my Enfield... Man, that had been such an amazing experience!

Evidently, the thought was mutual, because Adi suddenly sat up and said ...well, you can guess what he said.

'LET'S GO FOR A RIDE!'

The Amigos shall ride again!

Before you go…

Thanks so much for reading this book! You can check out all photos and our route map and various other stuff on the website - www.ketanjoshi.net

If you liked this book, please do leave a review on Amazon and Goodreads and share this book with your friends on Facebook, Twitter and any other networks you like - we self published authors need all the help we can get

My other books :

Fiction

Short story collections :

Bombay Mixture
Bombay High
Bombay Special

Detective stories

Dipy Singh - Private detective
Keep calm - and screw the boss (featuring Dipy Singh)

Non Fiction

Management

What they didn't teach you about Marketing.

Made in the USA
San Bernardino, CA
25 July 2017